LUKE

REFORMED EXPOSITORY BIBLE STUDIES

A Companion Series to the Reformed Expository Commentaries

Series Editors

Daniel M. Doriani
Iain M. Duguid
Richard D. Phillips
Philip Graham Ryken

1 Samuel: A King after God's Own Heart
Esther & Ruth: The Lord Delivers and Redeems
Daniel: Faith Enduring through Adversity
Matthew: Making Disciples for the Nations (two volumes)
Luke: Knowing for Sure (two volumes)
Galatians: The Gospel of Free Grace
Ephesians: The Glory of Christ in the Life of the Church
Hebrews: Standing Firm in Christ
James: Portrait of a Living Faith

Coming in 2022

Song of Songs: Friendship on Fire
John: The Word Incarnate (two volumes)
Philippians: To Live Is Christ

LUKE

KNOWING FOR SURE
Volume 2 (Chapters 11–24)

A 13-LESSON STUDY

REFORMED EXPOSITORY
BIBLE STUDY

JON NIELSON
and PHILIP GRAHAM RYKEN

PUBLISHING
P.O. BOX 817 • PHILLIPSBURG • NEW JERSEY 08865-0817

Scripture quotations are from the ESV® Bible (The Holy Bible, English Standard Version®), copyright © 2001 by Crossway, a publishing ministry of Good News Publishers. Used by permission. All rights reserved.

Unless otherwise indicated, boxed quotations are taken from Philip Graham Ryken's *Luke*, vol. 2, in the Reformed Expository Commentary series, and the page numbers in these quotations refer to that source.

The boxed quotations in lessons 1 and 2 are taken from volume 1 of Philip Graham Ryken's *Luke*, in the same series, and their page numbers (and accompanying volume number) refer instead to that source.

The quoted phrase in the boxed quotation on page 43 is from R. Kent Hughes, *Luke: That You May Know the Truth*, Preaching the Word (Wheaton, IL: Crossway, 1998), 2:111.

ISBN: 978-1-62995-844-6 (pbk)
ISBN: 978-1-62995-845-3 (ePub)

Printed in the United States of America

CONTENTS

SERIES INTRODUCTION

Studying the Bible will change your life. This is the consistent witness of Scripture and the experience of people all over the world, in every period of church history.

King David said, "The law of the LORD is perfect, reviving the soul; the testimony of the LORD is sure, making wise the simple; the precepts of the LORD are right, rejoicing the heart; the commandment of the LORD is pure, enlightening the eyes" (Ps. 19:7–8). So anyone who wants to be wiser and happier, and who wants to feel more alive, with a clearer perception of spiritual reality, should study the Scriptures.

Whether we study the Bible alone or with other Christians, it will change us from the inside out. The Reformed Expository Bible Studies provide tools for biblical transformation. Written as a companion to the Reformed Expository Commentary, this series of short books for personal or group study is designed to help people study the Bible for themselves, understand its message, and then apply its truths to daily life.

Each Bible study is introduced by a pastor-scholar who has written a full-length expository commentary on the same book of the Bible. The individual chapters start with the summary of a Bible passage, explaining **The Big Picture** of this portion of God's Word. Then the questions in **Getting Started** introduce one or two of the passage's main themes in ways that connect to life experience. These questions may be especially helpful for group leaders in generating lively conversation.

Understanding the Bible's message starts with seeing what is actually there, which is where **Observing the Text** comes in. Then the Bible study provides a longer and more in-depth set of questions entitled **Understanding the Text**. These questions carefully guide students through the entire passage, verse by verse or section by section.

It is important not to read a Bible passage in isolation, but to see it in the wider context of Scripture. So each Bible study includes two **Bible Connections** questions that invite readers to investigate passages from other places in Scripture—passages that add important background, offer valuable contrasts or comparisons, and especially connect the main passage to the person and work of Jesus Christ.

The next section is one of the most distinctive features of the Reformed Expository Bible Studies. The authors believe that the Bible teaches important doctrines of the Christian faith, and that reading biblical literature is enhanced when we know something about its underlying theology. The questions in **Theology Connections** identify some of these doctrines by bringing the Bible passage into conversation with creeds and confessions from the Reformed tradition, as well as with learned theologians of the church.

Our aim in all of this is to help ordinary Christians apply biblical truth to daily life. **Applying the Text** uses open-ended questions to get people thinking about sins that need to be confessed, attitudes that need to change, and areas of new obedience that need to come alive by the power and influence of the Holy Spirit. Finally, each study ends with a **Prayer Prompt** that invites Bible students to respond to what they are learning with petitions for God's help and words of praise and gratitude.

You will notice boxed quotations throughout the Bible study. These quotations come from one of the volumes in the Reformed Expository Commentary. Although the Bible study can stand alone and includes everything you need for a life-changing encounter with a book of the Bible, it is also intended to serve as a companion to a full commentary on the same biblical book. Reading the full commentary is especially useful for teachers who want to help their students answer the questions in the Bible study at a deeper level, as well as for students who wish to further enrich their own biblical understanding.

The people who worked together to produce this series of Bible studies have prayed that they will engage you more intimately with Scripture, producing the kind of spiritual transformation that only the Bible can bring.

Philip Graham Ryken
Coeditor of the Reformed Expository Commentary series
Author of *Luke* (REC)

INTRODUCING LUKE

Luke is the third and longest of the biblical Gospels. Its **main purpose** is to provide a true and orderly account of Christ's life, ministry, sufferings, death, and resurrection so that people who read the book "may have certainty concerning the things" (Luke 1:4) that it teaches about the Savior who came "to seek and to save the lost" (19:10). In other words, the gospel of Luke was written to strengthen our faith in Jesus and to give us greater assurance of the salvation he brings.

"The Gospel of Knowing for Sure," as we might call it, is named for the man who wrote it: "Luke the beloved physician" (Col. 4:14). Dr. Luke, who accompanied the apostle Paul on some of his famous missionary journeys, happens to be the only New Testament **author** who was not a Jew but a Greek. His careful attention to detail, tender compassion for people who suffer, and evident fascination with healing miracles all reflect his calling to the medical profession. Like many good Christian doctors, Luke was an everyday evangelist who wanted everyone he met to know more about Jesus. A gifted historian as well as a skilled physician, he penned not one but two best sellers—the New Testament book of Acts also bears his signature. In his gospel, Luke wrote down "all that Jesus began to do and teach" (Acts 1:1). Then, in the book of Acts, he told the rest of the story, portraying the good news of Jesus Christ being proclaimed all over the world through the power of the Holy Spirit.

Luke addressed both his gospel and its sequel to a person whom he calls "most excellent Theophilus" (Luke 1:3; see also Acts 1:1). Because he is given this honorific title ("most excellent"), some notable scholars maintain that Theophilus was a high-ranking Roman official. Since Luke's purpose behind what he wrote to Theophilus was to give greater assurance concerning the truth about Jesus, presumably this important leader was at least somewhat familiar with Christianity but wanted to learn more. Others believe that Luke wrote for Theophilus the son of Ananias, who became high priest in Jerusalem several years after Jesus died and rose again. But even though he was writing to a specific individual, Luke also had a more general **audience** in mind. The name *Theophilus* means "friend of God" or "lover of God." If we are friends of God through our loving faith in Jesus Christ, then this gospel was written for us as much as it was written for anyone.

Our understanding of Luke's audience makes a difference regarding how we understand the book's **context**. Was Luke writing to a Jew or a Gentile? To a religious leader in Jerusalem or to a Roman official in a city like Antioch—or even Rome itself? When we read this gospel, we discover that Luke provides sufficient information about daily life in ancient Galilee and religious customs in biblical Jerusalem for us to be able to understand Christ's life and ministry within their original setting.

Luke begins his account of Christ's public ministry with Jesus's first sermon, which he preached at his hometown synagogue in Nazareth. The book's **key verse** comes from Jesus's quotation from the Old Testament book of Isaiah: "The Spirit of the Lord is upon me, because he has anointed me to proclaim good news to the poor. He has sent me to proclaim liberty to the captives and recovering of sight to the blind, to set at liberty those who are oppressed, to proclaim the year of the Lord's favor" (Luke 4:18–19; cf. Isa. 61:1–2). Once he had read these words aloud, Jesus sat down and calmly said, "Today this Scripture has been fulfilled in your hearing" (Luke 4:21). By saying this, he was claiming to be the Savior whom God had always promised to send—the one who would preach good news to poor sinners and would bring healing for every wound and freedom from every form of bondage. As the rest of the gospel story unfolds, we will see Jesus actively carry out the exact kind of ministry that Isaiah foretold—one that was "mighty in deed and word" (24:19). He will heal the sick, give sight to the blind, set captives free from spiritual bondage, and—most of all—preach the good news of forgiveness for sin.

Many scholars have identified spiritual themes and specific episodes within the life of Christ that are unique to Luke's gospel. Luke gives us the fullest account of Jesus's birth and boyhood—one that includes four of the first Christmas carols. Of the gospel writers, he provides the most complete record of the healing ministry that Jesus exhibited as the Great

Physician. He tells more stories about forgiveness and places a special focus on prayer—eleven of the fifteen prayers of Jesus that are recorded in the Bible are included in Luke's gospel. He also retells nearly twenty parables about the kingdom of God that do not appear in the gospels of Matthew, Mark, or John—including many that deal with the stewardship of money and treat it as an important spiritual issue. And he takes special notice of the women who supported Jesus and were blessed by his ministry.[1]

As we encounter these varied episodes from the life of Christ, what **theological themes** can we discern within Luke's gospel? By providing the fullest account of our Savior's nativity—which includes the beautiful songs that men, women, and angels sang to celebrate his miraculous birth in Bethlehem—this gospel helps us to understand the mystery of the *incarnation*. Luke's down-to-earth presentation of the life of Christ generally emphasizes our Savior's humanity. But, paradoxically, his favorite title for Jesus—"Son of Man"—is an Old Testament term that bears witness to his deity.

Luke has even more to say about the death of Christ than he does about the birth of Christ. As do the other gospels, this one pays disproportionate attention to the last week of our Savior's life, when unrelenting opposition to his ministry intensified his sufferings and resulted in his bloody crucifixion. Luke wants us to understand the doctrine of the *atonement*—the truth that, by dying in our place, Jesus paid the price of our sins and reconciled us to God.

We should also see Luke as a theologian of the Holy Spirit—especially when we take into account the second part of his two-volume masterpiece: the book of Acts. The good doctor was interested in what theologians call *pneumatology*: the study of the person and work of the third member of the Trinity. From the moment he was baptized in the Jordan River through the moment he walked out of the empty tomb, Jesus was empowered by the Holy Spirit.

One more area to mention that Luke's theology encompasses is *missiology*, which relates to the church's calling to proclaim the gospel to the

---

1. In order to maximize the time we spend on some of the passages and episodes that are unique to Luke's gospel and tied to these central themes, this study will not include an in-depth examination of *every* passage in the book. At times, you will be encouraged to read some sections of his gospel without answering specific questions about them.

whole world. During his life on earth, Jesus preached the good news to as many needy people as he could: poor shepherds, lonely widows, crooked businessmen, despised lepers, and foreigners who were outside the family of faith. As he reached out to people who were lost, Jesus was beginning to fulfill the prophecy that had been issued at his birth that he would bring salvation to "all peoples"—to Gentiles as well as to Jews (2:31; see also 32). This work would continue through his disciples, whom he commissioned to preach "repentance for the forgiveness of sins . . . to all nations, beginning from Jerusalem" (24:47).

Every aspect of Luke's theology is designed not only to give us greater certainty about Christ's saving work but also to draw us deeper into the life of costly Christian discipleship. The most important **practical application** of his gospel we can make is simply to trust its message of salvation and to believe in Jesus. But that is not Luke's only objective for us: he also wants us to take up our crosses and follow Jesus.

One of Luke's favorite literary and pastoral techniques is to set two characters in contrast in order to demonstrate the true and best way to follow Jesus. Luke gives us two dinner guests, Simon and a sinful woman, along with opposite assessments of their spiritual condition (see 7:36–50); two sisters, Mary and Martha, who take different postures toward spiritual instruction (see 10:38–42); two brothers, younger and older, who were both far from their father's heart—but in very different ways (see 15:11–32); two neighbors from two different tax brackets, the rich man and poor Lazarus, who reached totally different eternal destinations (16:19–31); two men who went to the temple to pray, a Pharisee and a tax collector—only one of whom had a right standing with God (18:9–14); and so on.

True Christian disciples care for the same kinds of people whom Jesus treated with compassion. And if our Savior was both a healer of the body and a physician of the soul, then we too are called both to meet the material needs of our neighbors and to share the good news that may lead them to eternal life. By showing us how completely Jesus transformed the lives of the people he saved—how he liberated many people who were marginalized, oppressed, and underprivileged—Luke helps us to see the social implications of the gospel. The Savior whose miracles demonstrated his power over demons, disease, death, and the devil also calls us to see salvation in all its dimensions and to seek the lost by becoming the friends of sinners.

The gospel of Luke is not some tightly organized treatise but an evangelistic biography that tells many different stories about Jesus. Simply by reading the book from beginning to end, we get drawn into the narrative flow of the birth, life, ministry, sufferings, death, and triumphant resurrection of Jesus. But Luke also leaves us some clues to the fact that he has given careful thought to his book's structure. A crucial moment comes near the end of chapter 9, where Luke tells us that "when the days drew near for [Jesus] to be taken up, he set his face to go to Jerusalem" (v. 51). From that point forward, Christ resolutely set his course toward the cross.

The overall movement of the book is also indicated by Jesus's statement of purpose to Zacchaeus the tax collector: "The Son of Man came to seek and to save the lost" (Luke 19:10). We see Jesus *seeking* the lost from the beginning of his public ministry, when he seeks out his first disciples and begins preaching the good news of the kingdom to the lost souls of Israel. The stories we see in chapter 15 about the lost sheep, the lost coin, and the lost sons are really about his loving pursuit of every lost sinner. By the end of Luke's gospel we also see Jesus *saving* the lost—specifically by dying for their sins and rising again. We catch an early glimpse of this saving work when he tells Zacchaeus, "Today salvation has come to this house" (19:9). And his salvation is more fully displayed on the cross, when he welcomes the thief who is dying on the cross next to him into paradise (see 23:32–43). As we read these gospel stories, Jesus is looking to find us, too—and then to save us forever.

With these key moments in mind, here is one helpful way for us to **outline** the gospel of Luke:

Prologue: Luke's Purpose (1:1–4)

The Advent of the Son of Man
    Birth of Jesus (1:5–2:21)
    Boyhood of Jesus (2:22–52)
    Baptism of Jesus (3:1–38)
    Temptation of Jesus (4:1–13)

The Ministry of the Son of Man
    Jesus Begins His Ministry (4:14–44)

Jesus Calls His Disciples (5:1–6:16)
Jesus Teaches and Performs Miracles (6:17–8:56)
Jesus Commissions His Disciples (9:1–50)

The Mission of the Son of Man on his Way to the Cross
Jesus in Samaria (9:51–10:37)
Jesus in Bethany and Judea (10:38–13:21)
Jesus Journeys to Jerusalem (13:22–17:10)
Jesus between Samaria and Galilee (17:11–18:34)
Jesus near Jericho (18:35–19:27)

The Death of the Son of Man
Triumphal Entry (19:28–44)
Temple Discourses (19:45–21:38)
Last Supper (22:1–38)
Betrayal, Arrest, and Trials (22:39–23:25)
Crucifixion and Burial (23:26–56)

The Triumph of the Son of Man
Resurrection Day (24:1–49)
Ascension Day (24:50–53)

Philip Graham Ryken
Coeditor of the Reformed Expository Commentary series
Coeditor of the Reformed Expository Bible Study series
Author of *Luke* (REC)

LESSON 1

JESUS THE TEACHER

Luke 11:1–12:12

THE BIG PICTURE

As we begin our study of the second part of Luke's gospel, we come to an extended section of Jesus's collected teachings. These teachings cover a variety of subjects, but we will see them raising a key contrast, throughout, between the path of *humble discipleship* and *hypocritical religiosity*. Jesus gently instructs his humble disciples as he calls them to pray, witness boldly, and have confidence in the Father's care. He also firmly rebukes the hypocritical religious leaders as he calls them out for their outward displays of religion, which mask hearts that reject God as well as others.

Jesus begins by teaching his disciples about prayer—he gives them a *model* for how to pray (often called the "Lord's Prayer") and then offers them an invitation to pray *boldly* as children of God (11:1–13). We then see Luke recording an example of the ongoing authority that Jesus has over evil spirits, which Jesus explains is evidence that the Son of God has truly entered the world (11:14–26).

The passage then highlights the contrast between Jesus's disciples and religious hypocrites, as Jesus speaks of the blessing that comes to those who repent and believe when they hear his Word as well as the judgment that comes to those who reject it (11:27–36). He goes on to issue a series of proclamations of woe and judgment on the hypocritical scribes and Pharisees, who heap heavy religious burdens on others while harboring hearts that are far from God and devoid of genuine love for those who are

15

in need (11:37–12:3). The passage ends as Jesus again addresses his faithful disciples and prepares them to encounter persecution and hardship as well as to be able to witness boldly in the midst of trial (12:4–12).

Read Luke 11:1–12:12.

GETTING STARTED

1. What are some of the biggest struggles that you face in your prayer life? What about prayer is most difficult for you? What experiences or emotions have characterized times of strong and fervent prayer during your life?

2. Why is it so easy for Christians to focus on outward appearances of religiosity? In what ways are you tempted to put on a spiritual *show* while hiding what's really going on in your inner life and heart?

The Way God Sees Us, pg. 1:629

The gospel . . . helps us see ourselves the way God sees us, so that it no longer matters very much what other people think. The hypocrite is always desperate for more recognition, but the gospel convinces us that nothing we do for God has any merit of its own. We want to see ourselves the way God sees us: as forgiven sinners, accepted in Christ.

OBSERVING THE TEXT

3. Throughout this passage, what right attitudes and actions does Jesus say should characterize his disciples? What attitude should they have toward God—especially as they pray to him?

4. List some hypocritical behaviors that Jesus identifies throughout the second half of Luke 11. What is Jesus's attitude regarding this kind of hypocrisy?

5. What does Jesus say throughout this passage about the suffering and hardship that his followers can expect? What encouragement does he offer them for times when they are in the midst of hardship—and even persecution?

UNDERSTANDING THE TEXT

6. Why do you think one of Jesus's disciples asked him how to pray (11:1)? What should we, as his followers today, learn from his own habits of prayer that are described in the Gospels? How would you expound on

the main points, or petitions, contained within the brief prayer that Jesus teaches his disciples to pray in 11:2–4?

7. What approach to God does Jesus urge his disciples to take when they pray (11:5–13)? What understanding of God does this approach rest on—and what makes this so encouraging for us as God's children?

8. What, according to Jesus's own words, does the authority that he has over demons and evil spirits communicate about his identity (11:14–23)? What does he say to refute the arguments and criticisms that are issued against his powerful ministry?

Our Generous King, pg. 1:591
Our Father God loves to be a King to us in giving: "He who did not spare his own Son but gave him up for us all, how will he not also with him graciously give us all things?" (Rom. 8:32). God has given us his generous invitation, offering us everything we need in Jesus Christ. The question is whether we will go to him and ask for what we need, seeking and knocking until he answers.

9. What does Jesus say in 11:27–28 is the path to ultimate blessing? Based on the example of Nineveh, what is the relationship between belief and repentance (11:29–32)? Why, according to him, will the men of Nineveh serve as "witnesses" against those of his generation who reject him and his gospel?

10. Note the context that 11:37–38 provides for the extended words of woe and warning that Jesus speaks against the scribes and the Pharisees. How does he respond when the lawyer tells him in 11:45 that he has offended his fellow teachers of the law? What are some of the central accusations that Jesus levels against the scribes, Pharisees, and lawyers?

11. What does Jesus's tone throughout 11:37–12:3 tell us about his attitude regarding hypocrisy as well as religion that is merely an outward show? What shift takes place in his tone when he speaks to his disciples about how his presence will be with them when they are arrested and oppressed (12:4–12)?

BIBLE CONNECTIONS

12. Read Acts 5:1–11, in which Luke describes the hypocrisy and sin of Ananias and Sapphira as well as the judgment they receive from God.

What similarities do you see between the lesson God teaches the early church through their example and the woes and warnings Jesus has been teaching in the passage that we are studying?

13. As Stephen's death drew near, the angry crowd looked at him and observed that his face was like "the face of an angel" (Acts 6:15). Stephen then proceeded to speak one of the most eloquent and piercing sermons in church history . . . just before he was stoned to death (Acts 7:2–60). Where do you see, throughout the account of his death, the beautiful fulfillment of what Jesus says to his disciples in Luke 12:4–12?

THEOLOGY CONNECTIONS

14. Prayer, according to answer 98 of the Westminster Shorter Catechism, is "an offering up of our desires unto God for things agreeable to his will, in the name of Christ, with confession of our sins, and thankful acknowledgment of his mercies." How does this definition support Jesus's teaching from Luke 11:1–13? Why should an understanding that God is our *Father* strengthen our confidence as we approach him in prayer?

15. Philip Ryken writes of the boldness of the Scottish Reformer John Knox and notes that someone remarked of Knox, upon his death, "Here lies one who feared God so much that he never feared the face of man."[1] How might Luke 12:4–12 have served to inspire men and women like John Knox throughout church history—especially when they faced suffering and death for the sake of the gospel? What effect do these promises from Jesus have on you today?

APPLYING THE TEXT

16. How can Jesus's teaching from this passage shape, change, and form your prayer life? Which aspects of your prayer life are most in need of growth? What foundational truths about prayer should motivate you to come before God?

17. As you consider your path of discipleship under Jesus, what about this passage most encourages you? What part of Jesus's teaching convicts you the most?

---

1. Quoted in William Barclay, *The Gospel of Luke* (Philadelphia: Westminster, 1956), 164, which is quoted in Philip Graham Ryken, *Luke*, vol. 1, *Chapters 1–12* (Phillipsburg, NJ: 2009), 648.

18. How can Jesus's warnings about the purely *outward* righteousness of the scribes and Pharisees serve to guide your own walk with God? What sins might these warnings be calling you to confess—both to God and to others in your community of faith?

PRAYER PROMPT

As you close a lesson that is full of rich teachings and warnings from Jesus, pray that God would give you a heart that is humble and soft to receive his Son and his Word. Ask him to guard you, through his Spirit, against the temptation to be hypocritical, judgmental, and legalistic. Pray that he would form in you a childlike faith and strengthen you to walk the path of discipleship no matter what trouble, suffering, or persecution it brings your way.

A Pure Heart for Jesus, pg. 1:630

This is what the gospel does. It gives you true spiritual life, so that you are no longer dead inside, but wonderfully, vitally alive. It delivers you from the hypocrisy of external religiosity and pretentious piety, so that you can live with a clean, pure heart for Jesus. Only this kind of heart can offer the life of Christ to anyone else.

LESSON 2

THE RICH FOOL AND YOUR TREASURE

Luke 12:13–59

THE BIG PICTURE

Many biblical scholars have pointed out how often Luke's gospel records teaching from Jesus on the theme of *money* and *possessions*. As we see all throughout this gospel, Jesus welcomes the poor in spirit, who are despised and lowly, into his glorious kingdom—a kingdom that so often operates according to values that contrast with the world's common ways of thinking. In this lesson's passage, you will see Jesus teaching his disciples about the right approach to treasure as well as reminding them how foolish it is to grasp at treasure that does not last.

In response to a request he receives to adjudicate a dispute over an earthly inheritance, Jesus relates a parable about a "rich fool"—a man who makes great plans to attain earthly treasure, possessions, and future leisure (12:13–21). As this foolish man in the parable boasts proudly about his future, God responds by demanding his life from him. By telling us this parable, Jesus is issuing a call for us to be "rich toward God" rather than to focus on laying up treasure for ourselves on earth.

Jesus's teaching then moves on to address the temptations his disciples feel about being anxious and worried over possessions, money, and food (12:22–31). He cites the care that God shows to even the birds and wildflowers and reminds his disciples to seek after God's kingdom above all else.

He concludes the passage by again guiding his people to pursue eternal treasure, which can never be stolen or taken away from them (12:32–34). He also urges his disciples to stay ready and vigilant—to fear God and love their neighbors—in light of the day of the Lord, which will come unexpectedly (12:35–59).

Read Luke 12:13–59.

GETTING STARTED

1. Why do you think that Jesus's teaching so often concerns money and possessions? Does that seem odd to you? Why or why not?

2. What are some temptations related to money, possessions, and wealth that could inhibit someone's wholehearted pursuit of Jesus Christ and of living a life of service to him? What are some of the particular struggles that *you* experience in relation to the way you think about, worry about, or use money?

A Threat to Our Satisfaction, pg. 1:660–61

The things of this world cannot make us live. In fact, to the extent that they pull us away from finding satisfaction in Christ, they only keep us from really living. They may give us a temporary lift—the surge of pleasure that comes when we get what we want. But watch out! Nothing in this world can give you life.

OBSERVING THE TEXT

3. What do you notice about the context that 12:13–14 gives for the parable and teaching that Jesus relates in this passage? What motivation perhaps lies behind the question that Jesus is asked regarding the inheritance? Why do you think he responds to this question in the way that he does?

4. What do you learn about the character and thought process of the "rich fool" in Jesus's parable? How would you describe him? What do you notice about the things he says—and how do they betray his arrogance and self-obsession?

5. What illustrations from the natural world does Jesus bring into the teaching he delivers in 12:22–31? What causes those images and reminders from nature to be such a helpful source of support for the point he is making to his disciples?

UNDERSTANDING THE TEXT

6. What makes it obvious that the plans of the "rich fool" are selfish, sinful, and arrogant (12:16–19)? What other, more godly and generous questions might he have asked as he considered his wealth and possessions? How do his words make the presence of idolatry evident—and what would you identify this man's idols as being?

7. How does God respond to what this rich fool says—and what answer does his final question to him imply (12:20)? What does Jesus mean by the conclusion he offers to this parable (12:21)? What is the main lesson that he wants his disciples to learn from it?

8. Why do you think Jesus needed to encourage his disciples not to be anxious regarding clothing and food (12:22–23)? How do you see similar anxieties manifesting themselves in our lives today?

> **Irony, pg. 1:663**
> How ironic that a man who thinks he will live for many years is down to his last few hours on earth! How ironic that a man who wants to keep it all for himself will have to leave it all behind. And how ironic that a man who gives not one thought to God must still answer to God for his very soul.

9. What truths about the care that God shows his people does Jesus teach his disciples through the example of the birds and the lilies (12:24–27)? How can the oversight and care that God displays for the natural world remind us of his far deeper care for his redeemed children—and how can it encourage us not to worry or be anxious?

10. Note how Jesus seeks to shape the priorities of his people while still acknowledging the realities of their daily needs (12:29–31). Where should disciples of Jesus place their focus, passions, and chief concern?

11. What two kinds of treasure does Jesus contrast in 12:32–34? What is striking about the commands he gives his disciples regarding their wealth and generosity—and why is it important for Christians to wrestle with these commands?

BIBLE CONNECTIONS

12. Read Philippians 4:6—a verse in which the apostle Paul steers God's people away from anxiety and worry. Why must prayer play an important part in the battle we fight against worry, anxiety, and concerns regarding our possessions and provision? How does prayer help us in this battle?

13. In a verse that is often misquoted, the apostle Paul writes that "the love of money is a root of all kinds of evils" (1 Timothy 6:10). What inspiration might Paul have taken from Jesus's teaching in this passage as he made that statement? Why is it important to distinguish that it's the "love" of money—not money itself—that is the "root" of sin, evil, and idolatry?

THEOLOGY CONNECTIONS

14. Central to the tradition of Reformed theology are the doctrines of the *sovereignty* and *providence* of God—the truths that remind us that God rules and reigns over everything that comes to pass in the world and in our lives. What makes it obvious that the "rich fool" in Jesus's parable neglected these doctrines and instead sought to make himself his own sovereign god?

15. As many scholars have noted, the Bible is not against money or possessions; indeed, Luke writes about many wealthy patrons and homeowners in the book of Acts and shows them to be godly examples. What principles from this lesson's passage should guide the approach that followers of Jesus take to money and the accumulation of wealth and possessions?

APPLYING THE TEXT

16. What echoes of the heart and plans of the "rich fool" do you see within the plans, schemes, and intentions of people around you today? Where do you see his same arrogant attitude emerging in your own heart?

17. What antidotes does this passage prescribe to anxiety and worry regarding money? How can you, with the Spirit's help, seek to trust God more deeply in this area and invest in Christ's eternal kingdom more generously?

18. How can this passage serve to tweak the way that you think about money and earthly possessions? What areas of your life—particularly those that relate to money and possessions—need to be brought more in line with the priorities of Christ's eternal kingdom?

Invested in Heaven, pg. 1:678
Our earthly investments are subject to depreciation, loss, theft, and liquidation. But whatever we invest in the kingdom of God is safe forever. When we give to gospel work—especially to the poor—our funds are transferred directly to heaven, where they are exchanged for the currency of glory.

PRAYER PROMPT

As you close your study of this passage, pray for God to confront you and expose your heart's tendencies to love money—as well as your temptations to be anxious about money, possessions, and financial security. Ask him to give you a new perspective on these issues—one that is shaped by the principles of the eternal kingdom of your Savior, Jesus Christ, and that compels you to invest most fervently and passionately in treasures that reflect his glory. Pray that God would give you a generous heart, loosen your grip on your earthly treasure, and deepen your commitment to pursue his own eternal treasure.

LESSON 3

TRUE AND FALSE ISRAEL

Luke 13:1–35

THE BIG PICTURE

Many Jews in Jesus's day assumed that being an ethnic part of Israel meant that they were also part of the family and kingdom of God. As we see Jesus going on to continue his healing and teaching ministry, however, we will see him make one point abundantly clear: his kingdom is comprised of those who repent of their sin, put their faith in him, and bear real fruit as they live lives of obedience and worship. The kingdom of Jesus is available to all—and yet few will enter through its narrow door of faith and repentance.

The passage we will study for this lesson begins as Jesus corrects a common misconception: that bad things happen only to bad people and are intended as punishment for their sin (13:1–5). He says that the lesson his disciples should instead take away from tragedies is that everyone who does not repent will face ultimate punishment. The parable that he then tells and the healing he performs both illustrate the barrenness of the faith of many people in Israel—and even of the religious leaders—who miss the beauty of God's kingdom because of their insistence on legalism and tradition (13:6–17). In the parable, Jesus compares Israel to a fig tree that bears no fruit; and the healing, which he performs for a woman, is met by resistance from the ruler of the synagogue because it occurs on the Sabbath—proving his point that an obsession with keeping laws will choke out a person's potential for fruitful and loving faith.

Jesus then continues to teach about his eternal kingdom by comparing it to a mustard seed and then to leaven—both of which spread and grow in surprising ways (13:18–21). He also says that the kingdom of God will be difficult to enter—that it is like a narrow door through which some go but many cannot (13:22–30). And, in fact, many people from the community of Israel continue to refuse to repent and enter this narrow door through faith in Jesus, which causes him to lament and weep over these people he loves (13:31–35). The true Israel of God, according to Jesus, is made up of men and women from all nations who humbly repent, trust the Messiah, and bear fruit in accordance with their faith.

Read Luke 13:1–35.

GETTING STARTED

1. What might lead people in your culture today to *assume* that God is pleased with them or that they will be accepted into heaven after they die?

   By refraining from obviously evil deeds; by achieving status in their endeavors; from prosperity from professional success. And by NOT understanding God's holiness + holy hatred of any deviation of tho't, word + deed by His moral perfection.

2. Why do people often accuse Christianity (as well as Christians themselves) of being exclusive, judgmental, or narrow-minded? In what ways can those accusations be legitimate and truthful? In what ways do you see some of those accusations being leveled unfairly or without a full understanding of the Bible's teaching?

   We often "judge" certain sins and zero in on them w/o offering an understanding of sin as mankind's problem. Choosing certain sins, eg. homosexuality, and focusing on damnation for it (speck in others' eye + log in our own), we stand apart from others as superior — w/o repenting of our own sinfulness + misrepresentation of gospel of grace thru X.

Exclusive and Inclusive, pg. 49

In one sense, Christianity is the most *exclusive* of all religions. According to Jesus himself, there is only one narrow way of salvation. Those who find it are included; everyone else is excluded. But in another sense, Christianity is the most *inclusive* of all religions. . . . You just have to be a sinner who is praying for God to give you grace in Jesus Christ.

OBSERVING THE TEXT

3. What are some of the main *contrasts* that this passage draws between people who are part of the kingdom of God and people who are not?

v.17, humiliated but not humbled!

4. What key roles do Pharisees and Jewish religious leaders return to play throughout this passage? Describe the way they respond to Jesus. What rebukes and warnings does he issue to them in the passage?

tradition — Consistency in their hypocrisy — they hold to the law but lacking the heart of obedience

W/o repentance they will perish.

5. How does this passage display the heart that Jesus has for sinners? Where do you see him showing anger and disappointment throughout it? Where does he display his tenderness and mercy?

UNDERSTANDING THE TEXT

6. What views of suffering and tragedy do the disciples seem to have embraced, based on what Jesus says in Luke 13:1–5? What does he do to correct their thinking and adjust their perspective?

7. What lesson is Jesus's parable about the barren fig tree intended to teach—and toward whom does it seem to be directed (13:6–9)? What does the ruler of the synagogue reveal about the condition of his heart through the way he responds when Jesus heals the woman with the disabling spirit (13:10–17)? What does Jesus demonstrate that he values even more than Sabbath traditions and rules?

8. What do the brief parables that Jesus relates in 13:18–21 reveal about the nature of God's kingdom? What new understanding did they offer the disciples about the kind of kingdom that Jesus was bringing into the world?

9. What about Jesus's teaching regarding the "narrow door" and the difficulty of entering the kingdom of God should serve to awaken his audience to their need for repentance and faith (13:22–28)? Why might his words have surprised those who considered themselves to be safe and secure because of their Jewish heritage?

Confession, Contrition, Change, pg. 7

Have you repented in the biblical way? Confession is the intellectual aspect of repentance: we know in our minds that we have sinned. Contrition is the emotional aspect of repentance: we feel in our hearts that we have sinned. Change is the volitional aspect of repentance: we resolve in our wills that we will go and sin no more. All three aspects are essential for our repentance to be genuine.

10. Notice the surprising themes of *inclusion* that appear in Jesus's words in 13:29–30. What will be surprising about who is included in the kingdom of God? About who is *excluded* from it? What reversals will take place within this kingdom?

11. How does Luke 13:31–35 foreshadow Jesus's crucifixion? How does it reveal the longing he feels, even as he considers his own death, for those who reject him to repent and experience a change of heart? What encourages you about these verses?

BIBLE CONNECTIONS

12. In Galatians 5:22–23, the apostle Paul describes the "fruit of the Spirit"—fruit that should grow from the lives of followers of Jesus. How do these verses help to explain the parable of the fig tree that Jesus tells in Luke 13:6–9? How does the ruler of the synagogue reveal his own lack of spiritual fruit through the way he responds to Jesus's healing of the suffering woman in 13:10–17?

13. Read 2 Peter 3:9–10. What themes that arise from what the apostle Peter says about God's patient heart connect beautifully with the lament that Jesus voices over Jerusalem at the end of the passage we are studying today? How can these verses from 2 Peter help you to better understand the purposes and timing that God operates according to as the return of Jesus draws nearer?

THEOLOGY CONNECTIONS

14. According to Jesus, the narrow door of the kingdom of God can be entered only through genuine *repentance* of sin. The Westminster Confession of Faith describes repentance this way: "A sinner, out of the sight and sense, not only of the danger, but also of the filthiness and odiousness of his sins, as contrary to the holy nature and righteous law of God . . . so grieves for and hates his sins as to turn from them all unto God, purposing . . . to walk with him in all the ways of his commandments" (15.2). Which of those specific aspects of repentance stand out to you? Which of its aspects do we sometimes tend to omit when we are repenting?

15. The language of the "narrow door" from Luke 13:24 speaks to the Christian doctrine of the *exclusivity of Christ*—the truth that salvation comes through faith in Christ *alone*, to the exclusion of all other religious systems, teachings, or saviors. Why is it so important for followers of

Jesus to protect this doctrine—and what would be lost if this doctrine were abandoned?

APPLYING THE TEXT

16. How should Jesus's teaching from Luke 13:1–5 shape the way we interpret God's purposes when accidents, tragedies, and disasters happen? What ultimate, eternal realities and responsibilities should such events lead us to consider?

17. What truths regarding our salvation should Jesus's teaching about the "narrow door," which few will enter, cause us to remember? What should this teaching cause us to evaluate within our own hearts?

There Is Still Time, pg. 61
What happened to Jerusalem will happen to any nation, city, church, or individual who refuses to find safety in Christ. If we will not come to him, we will be forsaken by God, and eventually we will be destroyed. Yet there is still time for us to come to him by faith. There is still time for us to come under the safety of his wings.

18. What do the final verses of this passage (13:31–35) remind you regarding the heart that Jesus has for sinners who are far from him? Why should this reminder encourage you—and how might these verses spur you on to evangelize and witness lovingly to those who seem to be far from faith in Christ?

PRAYER PROMPT

This passage shows us some difficult, albeit beautiful, truths about the kingdom of God. The door into it is narrow—and many will refuse to enter it because of their resistance against repentance, humility, and the path of discipleship. Yet all who repent of sin, place their faith in Jesus, and follow him alone are welcome within the family of God! Today, praise God for the wonderful exclusivity of his kingdom—a kingdom into which you yourself have entered if you have put your faith in his Son. Ask God to grant you the grace to share in the merciful heart Jesus has for sinners—who still have the time and opportunity to turn to the Messiah.

LESSON 4

THE GREAT WEDDING FEAST

Luke 14:1–35

THE BIG PICTURE

The setting of the entire passage that we will study next is a feast that a wealthy leader of the Pharisees is hosting in his home and has invited Jesus to attend (14:1). As Jesus heals a suffering man, teaches the group, and questions his host and the other influential guests, he confronts them yet again with surprising truths about his kingdom: the poor are welcome, and the last will be first. God's people are called to lovingly welcome those who are lowly and weak in the eyes of the world.

Jesus begins by placing a man who is afflicted with dropsy before the Pharisees and religious leaders who have gathered in the house and then confronting them with a familiar question: Is it right for him to heal this man on the Sabbath day (14:1–6)? When the religious leaders respond only with silence, Jesus heals the man—before reminding the Pharisees that they would work to help even an *animal* that belonged to them, if it stumbled or became stuck on the Sabbath. Jesus then shifts into teaching—he lays out the context of a great wedding feast and refers to the common custom of guests jostling and competing for the seats of highest honor (14:7–11). According to Jesus, true disciples of God do the opposite: they refuse the urge to "exalt" themselves and opt rather to humble themselves and honor others instead. Similarly, his command when his servants are *hosting* a banquet is to invite the poor, the lowly, the lame—not the rich, who will be able to turn and repay the host (14:12–14). The passage concludes with a longer parable that Jesus tells to explain God's determination to move past those who proudly reject him (as many of the religious leaders have) and to welcome those who are poor, lowly, and rejected in the eyes of the world (14:15–24). God's call to his great salvation banquet will move outward from Israel to the "highways and hedges" of the nations as it welcomes repentant Gentile sinners in (v. 23). Jesus ends by reminding those who seek to embrace him and share in his salvation banquet that the cost of discipleship is great—that they must count this cost of following him (14:25–35).

Read Luke 14:1–35.

GETTING STARTED

1. How do you see the impulse of self-exaltation being played out in the lives, words, and pursuits of people around you? Why are people so desperate for recognition, praise, and fame?

2. What are some examples of "good deeds" that people may do out of deeply selfish motivations? Why is it much more difficult for us to serve or give to people or causes when we know there will be no recognition, repayment, or reward for doing so?

Don't Refuse the Banquet, pg. 87
Heed his warning! The Savior is here. His banquet is ready. There is still room at his table. But if we are so foolish as to refuse his open invitation—no matter what excuse we make—it is not just dinner that we will miss, but our very salvation. Do not miss out on what Jesus wants to give you, but come when you are called!

OBSERVING THE TEXT

3. What does Luke tell us about the context for the healing and teaching that we read about from Jesus in this passage (14:1)? Why is this context important to our understanding of the main emphasis of his teaching and of the repeated metaphors that he uses in his parables?

4. How would you characterize the Pharisees' behavior and the responses they give to Jesus throughout this passage? Do they seem to be learning and to be accepting his teaching? Or do they seem resistant to it?

5. What are some of the ways that Jesus says the values of his kingdom reverse the values of the world? Which of the common impulses and pursuits of selfish human beings does he turn upside down when he calls us to follow him?

UNDERSTANDING THE TEXT

6. What does Jesus again teach the Pharisees about the Sabbath day, and about the heart of God, as he heals the man with dropsy in 14:1–6? Why do you think they are unable to respond to the question Jesus asks them in 14:5–6?

7. What natural human tendency and desire does Jesus forcefully confront in 14:7–11? What makes this tendency so out of step with the values of Jesus and his kingdom (14:11)? What can the way in which he confronts this tendency teach us about the perspective that God has of the world—as well as about what we can expect when we are before his throne on the day of judgment?

8. What can we conclude about the motivations that lay behind invitations, gifts, and acts of kindness that were offered in Jesus's day (14:12)? In what ways do you see these same motivations at play today? What selfish incentives can lie behind what seem to be acts of generosity and kindness—and what can help us to be aware of them?

9. How *should* followers of Jesus perform acts of kindness and love—and what should motivate them to do so (14:13–14)? Why are the commands that Jesus gives us in this area often so difficult for us to follow?

10. Notice the comment that is voiced by one of the religious leaders (14:15) and that leads Jesus to give his parable about the banquet. What seems to be the tone, or intent, of this exclamation? How does the beginning of Jesus's parable (14:16–20) illustrate the fact that the intent behind the comment was mistaken? What demonstrates for us that many of these religious leaders from Jesus's day are continuing to refuse the invitation that God offers through his Son?

11. What might the second round of invitations to the banquet that Jesus describes going out in 14:21–24 be serving to teach us about the kingdom of God? While it describes many people rejecting the offer and says that they will not taste the banquet, who does the parable say *will* ultimately attend the feast—and what makes this tremendously good news for us today?

Judgment for the Self-Exalting, pg. 71

For people who exalt themselves—who think they are good enough to stand before God on their own merits—the final judgment will be a total humiliation. People like the Pharisees, who believe in "salvation by recognition," will not get what *they* think they deserve; they will get what *God* thinks they deserve.

BIBLE CONNECTIONS

12. As Jesus declares that the lowly will be exalted, we cannot help but recognize that the reversal he is describing is most beautifully reflected in the example of his own life and ministry—his incarnation, death, resurrection, ascension, and reign. Read Philippians 2:1–11. How does Jesus himself provide an example of the life that we should expect to live as followers of God? What must we remember about the ultimate reward and exaltation that await Christ and his people?

13. Read 2 Corinthians 5:20, in which the apostle Paul makes an appeal to his readers in his capacity as a minister of God's reconciliation. How do we embody the invitations to the banquet that Jesus described in his parable when we proclaim the gospel? How are God's people today called to make this invitation?

THEOLOGY CONNECTIONS

14. Luke 14:11 reminds us of the positive example of Jesus, who was humbled on the cross before being exalted as Savior and King forever. But this verse also alerts us to the opposite reversal that will take place on the day of judgment for those who exalt themselves in opposition to God and reject his Son—such people will go from a place of exaltation to one of humiliation. Why is it important for us to continue to teach the doctrine of the *final judgment* of sinners as well as the reality of hell and eternal punishment? How can this doctrine accompany our proclamation of the gospel of forgiveness and grace that is available for

those who humbly repent? Why must we include this doctrine in our evangelizing?

15. John Calvin writes, "As the surest source of destruction to men is to obey themselves, so the only haven of safety is to have no other will, no other wisdom, than to follow the Lord wherever he leads. Let this, then, be the first step, to abandon ourselves, and devote the whole energy of our minds to the service of God" (*Institutes*, 3.7.1). How does the difficult teaching that Jesus delivers in this passage serve to call his followers to "abandon" themselves and obey him?

APPLYING THE TEXT

16. When are you tempted to jostle for position and pursue recognition instead of humbly exalting others? What sinful attitudes might your tendency to do so be revealing in your heart—and what can you do to confront those attitudes and confess them to God?

Our Humble God—Our Example, pg. 73
Where do we learn to live and to love with this kind of humility? We learn it from the Son of God, who took the very lowest place that anyone has ever taken, and as a result, is now exalted to the highest place in the universe.

17. What acts of love, kindness, and welcome have you offered to those whom you know can repay you or bring you some kind of benefit? How can you fight against the tendency to focus your efforts on people like this and instead serve people more frequently who cannot repay you?

18. Why is it dangerous to try to live out Jesus's commands in this passage—regarding service, humility, and welcoming the poor—without first submitting to Jesus himself in repentance and faith? Why must we accept Jesus as our Savior before we can make him our example?

PRAYER PROMPT

This is a passage that calls us to confront—and reverse—many of the tendencies that come so naturally to us as sinful and selfish people. We are called, as Jesus leads us and the Holy Spirit convicts and guides us, to exalt others rather than ourselves. We are called to welcome and care for others with no regard for what we will get in return. And we are called to humbly receive God's invitation to his kingdom and to live sacrificially for the Savior who gave himself as a sacrifice for us. Today, pray for God to give you his strength so that you can pursue attitudes, impulses, and actions that are focused on others! Ask his Holy Spirit to help you and lead you.

LESSON 5

THE PRODIGAL GOD

Luke 15:1-32

THE BIG PICTURE

In this lesson, you will study one of Jesus's most well-known parables—the story of the prodigal son, who leaves home in order to squander his inheritance, only to return to the surprisingly open arms of his gracious and forgiving father. This is a beautiful picture of the grace that God shows to rebellious sinners when they turn back to him in repentance and seek mercy and forgiveness from him through Christ. Yet even though this parable is well known, it is not often studied within the rest of the context of this chapter of Luke's gospel.

Luke 15 begins with yet another confrontation between Jesus and the Pharisees and scribes (15:1-2). As Jesus continues to teach, tax collectors and sinners draw near in order to hear him—much to the indignation of the Jewish religious leaders. The three parables that Jesus tells next make up his response to the hostile grumbling of the Pharisees and scribes, who are obviously failing to grasp the welcoming heart that God has for lost sinners. Jesus tells of a sheep, in a fold of a hundred, that becomes lost (15:3-7). Once the owner finds the lost sheep, he calls his friends together and rejoices. Similarly, when a woman in his next parable loses one of her ten silver coins, she searches for it until she finds it; when she does, she similarly invites her friends to rejoice and celebrate with her (15:8-10). Both parables illustrate the rejoicing that takes place in heaven over each individual lost sinner who repents (vv. 7, 10).

Jesus's third parable is much longer and more complex, but it again illustrates the beautiful reality of the rejoicing that occurs in heaven over sinners who repent and turn to the loving and gracious Father (15:11–32). The younger of two sons demands his inheritance from his father, proceeds to squander it entirely through reckless and sinful living, and ultimately returns home humbled and empty-handed. The father, upon seeing him from a long way off, welcomes him with celebration and feasting. As Jesus tells this third parable, though, he introduces another element: the sullen elder brother (vv. 25–32). The gracious father is forced to confront the bitterness and self-righteousness of this brother, who begrudges the kindness that the father is showing his other son—much as the Pharisees and scribes are grumbling about Jesus's ministry to tax collectors and sinners!

Read Luke 15:1–32.

GETTING STARTED

1. How do people—including Christians—try to minimize their sin, their need, and their deep brokenness apart from the grace of God? What factors cause us to consider ourselves to be basically "good" rather than desperately sinful and fallen?

Our Shepherd's Joy, pg. 112

Jesus wants us to share the joy that he has in finding the lost. We share our shepherd's joy when we admit that we have gone astray and need him to come and find us. We share his joy when we accept being found and ask him to carry us back home, and even more when we celebrate our salvation.

2. Why is self-righteousness in the community of faith such a turn-off for unchurched people? In what ways have you been guilty of self-righteousness or of seeing certain people as being beyond hope and out of the reach of God's grace?

OBSERVING THE TEXT

3. What is so important about the context that the opening of this chapter provides (15:1–2)? How does this confrontation at the beginning of the chapter shape our understanding of Jesus's purpose behind the three parables he tells and the audience for whom he intends them?

4. What does the structure of this chapter tell us about the purpose and main message behind what Jesus says in it? What are the basic elements of each of his three parables? What does Jesus *add* to the third parable?

5. What do you observe about the elder brother's character and about the response he gives to the celebration that is going on (15:27–32)? What might cause us to sympathize with his feelings and objections?

UNDERSTANDING THE TEXT

6. What do we learn about Jesus's ministry from the beginning of this passage (15:1)? Why might the Pharisees and scribes be reacting so negatively to his ministry—and what tone do you detect in their words (15:2)?

7. What is Jesus emphasizing by mentioning that the lost sheep in his parable in 15:3–7 was just one out of a flock of a hundred? How does the owner react when he finally finds the lost sheep (v. 6)? What does Jesus say about the way heaven responds to a lost sinner who repents (v. 7)?

8. What similarities does the parable of the lost coin have to the parable of the lost sheep (15:8–10)? How is Jesus again making a point about heaven's perspective on lost sinners and the proper way to respond to repentance and salvation (v. 10)?

Where the Pharisees Were Right, pg. 113
The Pharisees we meet in the Gospels were wrong about many things, including God's requirements for salvation and their own righteousness, and wrong about the true identity of Jesus Christ. But at least they were right about this: Jesus was a man who welcomed sinners. We know this because they said, "This man receives sinners and eats with them" (Luke 15:2).

9. How does the beginning of the third parable illustrate the rebellious-ness, selfishness, and sin of the younger son (15:11–16)? When the son comes to the end of himself, what makes it evident that he has had a change of heart and is demonstrating true humility and repentance (15:17–19)?

10. Notice the way that the father responds to the younger son as he hum-bly returns to him (15:20–24). How would you describe the welcome that he gives him? What is this meant to teach us about our heavenly Father?

11. Why is the elder brother angry at the celebratory welcome that the younger brother receives—and what makes this response somewhat understandable (15:25–30)? How does the father demonstrate grace and care for this elder brother as well as the younger (15:31–32)? How many of the sons in this story need God's gracious salvation—and why?

BIBLE CONNECTIONS

12. Read Ephesians 2:1–3. How does the apostle Paul describe the natural state we are in apart from the saving grace of Jesus Christ? Why is it so important for us to remember that these verses describe *each one* of us—no matter our heritage, upbringing, or family name?

13. Now read Ephesians 2:4–10. What makes the gospel such good news for sinners, according to these verses? What is God's ultimate and eternal purpose for *every sinner* who repents and turns to Jesus in faith?

THEOLOGY CONNECTIONS

14. The Westminster Confession of Faith explains that every sin "does, in its own nature, bring guilt upon the sinner; whereby he is bound over to the wrath of God, and curse of the law, and so made subject to death, with all miseries spiritual, temporal, and eternal" (6.6). How does the condition that the prodigal son winds up in, after squandering his inheritance, present a vivid picture of these truths about the effects of sin? Why must we see our own spiritual condition, apart from Christ, as being the same as his?

15. Philip Ryken quotes from J. C. Ryle in his commentary: "The man who really feels that we all stand by grace and are all debtors, and that the best of us has nothing to boast of, and has nothing which he has not received—such a man will not be found talking like the 'elder brother.'"[1] Why is having an understanding of our own depravity, and of the depth of God's amazing grace, our best defense against developing a heart that is like the elder brother's?

APPLYING THE TEXT

16. What do the parables from Luke 15 add to your understanding of the heart of your God? What does their description of the "rejoicing" that occurs in heaven when sinners repent do for your understanding of your own salvation—and of the salvation of others?

17. How can this chapter of Luke serve to spur on your passion and zeal for sharing the gospel of Jesus Christ? With what *kind* of people does this passage encourage you to share the message of Jesus?

1. J. C. Ryle, *Expository Thoughts on the Gospels: Luke* (1858; repr., Cambridge: James Clarke, 1976), 2:191, quoted in Philip Graham Ryken, *Luke*, vol. 2, *Chapters 13–24* (Phillipsburg, NJ: 2009), 163.

18. What do you find convicting about the Pharisees' and scribes' response to Jesus—and about the elder brother's response to the father? How do you see your own heart being reflected in these responses? How might you still need to grow to further embrace the merciful heart that God has for broken sinners?

PRAYER PROMPT

This passage leads us to rejoice in the gracious heart of our welcoming God. Take a moment, right now, to praise God for seeking and saving a lost sinner like you . . . and thank him for the fact that all heaven rejoiced the day that you turned to Jesus Christ in repentance and faith! But take time as well to examine before God your own tendencies to act like the elder brother in Jesus's third parable. Repent of your self-righteousness and of your failure to rejoice over God's pursuit of sinners who are no different from you. Pray for God to make your heart more and more like the heart that *he* has for the lost.

Lost and in Need of Grace, pg. 163
If only we could see how lost we are, even if we think we are living with the Father. If only we understood how much damage our self-righteousness does to our relationship with God. If only we learned how to repent of our supposed righteousness as well as our sinful depravity. If only we knew that we need as much grace as anyone does.

LESSON 6

THE RICH MAN AND LAZARUS

Luke 16:1–31

THE BIG PICTURE

As we saw in lesson 2 of this book, Luke records many occasions on which Jesus taught about the subject of money, wealth, and possessions—which some of us may find surprising. Obviously, however, both Luke and Jesus see this as an area of our lives that exposes our true allegiances and genuine objects of worship. Do we place our hope in our possessions or in the eternal inheritance that we have through Christ?

The passage for this lesson begins with a parable that Jesus tells about a crafty and dishonest manager (16:1–13). Knowing that he is about to be released from his duties, he quickly begins massively reducing the debts of his master's servants in order to earn favor with them so that they will care for him in the future. And his master actually commends him for his craftiness (v. 8)! Jesus's point behind telling this parable is that we often set ourselves up securely in this life—even going so far as to employ crafty means to do so—but fail to invest in our eternal future, which is much more valuable. Ultimately, no one can serve two masters; we must choose between loving and worshiping either God or our earthly wealth (v. 13). When the money-loving Pharisees respond to this parable with mockery, Jesus shows how their outward embrace of the law masks their inner sinfulness and greed (16:14–18).

We will spend most of this lesson on Jesus's striking account of the rich man and Lazarus (16:19–31). While speaking mainly to money-loving Pharisees, Jesus tells a story about a rich man who selfishly lives in luxury while ignoring the pleas of a poor beggar named Lazarus who lies each day at his gate. When the two men die, Lazarus is carried into the presence of God ("to Abraham's side") while the rich man begins to endure eternal punishment for his sin and unbelief, and there is a great "chasm" fixed between the two men (v. 26). The rich man begs Abraham to send Lazarus to warn his family of their impending judgment; Abraham, however, tells him that if they have not responded in faith to the words of Moses and the prophets, they will not believe a new messenger either (v. 30). This haunting account ends with an implicit call for us to respond to Jesus Christ with repentance and faith, to show joyful generosity to those in need, and to invest in our eternal future.

Read Luke 16:1–31.

GETTING STARTED

1. What signs and indications do you see that your culture treats money as an idol—as something to serve, worship, and cherish?

2. The love of money—which often comes across as an obsession with money—can invade people's lives and hearts, no matter how much of it they possess. What worries and anxieties arise from financial need? Conversely, what temptations accompany financial success and blessing?

Jesus Offers You Joy, pg. 179

Do not let money master you, but bring yourself and everything you have under the mastery of Jesus Christ. Remember how many riches he left behind to be your Savior. Remember his own great expense in giving his blood for your sins on the cross. . . . He is not trying to rob you of any joy, but to give you more joy by giving you more of himself.

OBSERVING THE TEXT

3. The parable of the dishonest manager could have had the potential to be difficult to understand had Jesus not explained it in 16:8–9. How do those verses help to make his point clear ?

4. How can verses 14–18 be seen as connecting that first parable to the account of the rich man and Lazarus? What do those verses reveal about the Pharisees' hearts as Jesus responds to them? What hint is verse 18 perhaps giving us about one more way these religious leaders were failing to keep God's law (besides loving money and failing to be generous)?

5. Note the contrasts that are laid out between the earthly lives and the eternal destinies of the rich man and of Lazarus (16:19–31). What sets them apart on earth? What sets them apart in the afterlife? What might be significant about even the fact that one of them is *named* while the other isn't?

UNDERSTANDING THE TEXT

6. What is despicable and selfish about the behavior of the dishonest manager in Jesus's parable from 16:1–9? As Jesus describes this behavior, what point is he making about our investment in our eternal future?

7. How does what Jesus goes on to say in 16:10–13 help us to further understand the point he was making through his parable about the dishonest manager? What does he say is the ultimate choice that faces each person regarding worship, service, and adoration (v. 13)?

8. Who does Luke 16:14 tell us was the immediate audience that Jesus's account of the rich man and Lazarus was intended for? In what way could 16:19–21 be seen as a picture of the Pharisees' lifestyle—and of their neglect of the poor? What makes this such a terrible incongruity—especially since they held the role of religious leaders of God's people?

9. What are the differences between the eternal destinies of these two men (16:22–26)? What comfort does Lazarus enjoy because of his faith? What torment does the rich man endure? What do we learn about

eternal joy—and punishment—through the response that Abraham gives to the rich man (vv. 25–26)?

10. Notice the plea that the rich man makes in 16:27–28. Why does he want a message to be sent to the members of his family? What truths does he understand now—albeit with eternal regret?

11. What does Abraham's answer to the rich man's plea teach us about human sin, stubbornness, and rebellion (16:29–31)? In what way does this parable implicitly invite *us* to respond to the warnings of judgment it contains, as well as the generous offer of salvation that comes through Jesus Christ? How does this account serve to remind us how urgent this gospel call is and how weighty our response to it is?

Riches Received by Faith, pg. 199

Although being poor does not save people any more than being rich does, it is still a great encouragement to see what riches the poor may receive by faith. When Lazarus died, the torment of his earthly troubles was over. Immediately he went to be with all the saints, the place Jesus described as resting on the bosom of Abraham. This symbolizes the blessed joy every believer has after death.

BIBLE CONNECTIONS

12. Read Psalm 112:1–6. How does the portrait of the righteous man that these verses paint demonstrate the way in which those who are blessed with worldly wealth can honor and glorify God?

13. Now read 1 Timothy 6:6–10. What dangers do money and worldly possessions introduce? Why is contentment such an important fruit of the work that the gospel does in the hearts of Jesus's followers?

THEOLOGY CONNECTIONS

14. The Westminster Confession of Faith reminds us that "God has appointed a day wherein he will judge the world in righteousness by Jesus Christ, to whom all power and judgment is given of the Father. In which day, not only the apostate angels shall be judged, but likewise all persons that have lived upon earth shall appear before the tribunal of Christ, to give an account of their thoughts, words, and deeds" (33.1). What does Jesus teach, in this passage we have been studying, about life after death and about judgment? Why should we think often about these realities?

15. John Calvin wrote, "It is not enough that my neighbors serve me, for God did not only create them for me. I must also acquit myself for my part, knowing that I was also created for them. Let me offer myself, and ask only to provide what I have received, so that there may be a reciprocal duty as our Lord has commanded. This is what we must do."[1] In what way was the rich man guilty of failing to live out these ideals?

APPLYING THE TEXT

16. How can the crafty "investment" that the dishonest manager made in his earthly future inspire us to make a more careful and worshipful investment in our eternal future? In what ways can even your worldly resources—your wealth and money—be used in the service of God's eternal purposes and glory, and what could you do to invest them in this way to a greater degree?

17. What do you find convicting as you read the account of the rich man and Lazarus? What tempts you to resist showing radical generosity— and why? How does your use of money serve to reflect your deepest priorities and desires—and even your worship?

---

1. John Calvin, "Sermon on 1 Cor. 11:11–16," in *Men, Women, and Order in the Church: Three Sermons*, trans. Seth Skolnitsky (Dallas: Presbyterian Heritage Publications, 1992), 48.

18. In what way must your approach to being generous and caring for others in this life be shaped by the sacrificial death of Jesus Christ and by God the Father's generous gift of salvation? Why must you base your approach to money, possessions, and generosity on the foundation of the truth of the gospel?

PRAYER PROMPT

This heavy passage should confront each one of us and make us ask probing questions about what receives our deepest love and our most fervent worship. Do we love our possessions and trust in our worldly wealth? Or do we treasure Christ above all and seek to invest in our eternal future with him? As you end your study of this passage, spend time asking God to help you to put your love of money and wealth to death by the power of his Spirit. Pray for him to enable you to treasure Christ your Savior more and more and to respond to others with sacrificial care, generosity, and compassion.

The Only Thing That Matters, pg. 198

Death is the great equalizer. As wealthy as he was, the rich man was just as likely to die as Lazarus was, because whether we are rich or poor, none of us can escape the cold hand of the grave. No matter how much money we have, it will never completely save our lives. Worldly wealth cannot prevent our own inevitable demise, and when it finally happens, the only thing that will matter is our relationship to God.

LESSON 7

THE PHARISEE AND
THE TAX COLLECTOR

Luke 17:1–19:27

THE BIG PICTURE

While we will not cover Luke 17 in this study, please read through that chapter, which contains more of Jesus's teaching about discipleship and service for God, his healing of a group of lepers, and his pointed predictions about the coming day of the Lord.

The passage that we *will* study in this lesson consists of two parables that Jesus tells in order to instruct his disciples regarding their *prayers*. On the one hand, God's people must approach him with boldness as they earnestly bring their requests before him and trust his faithfulness, grace, and fatherly love. On the other hand, they also come to God as sinners in need of his mercy and bow before him in reverence, awe, and worship—thus, the prayers of God's people must reflect deep humility as well.

Jesus's first parable describes how a widow pursues justice from the judge of her city, who is godless and unjust (18:1–8). Even though this judge neither fears God nor respects man, he eventually gives justice to the widow because of her dogged persistence (vv. 4–5). Jesus's argument moves from the lesser to the greater as he reminds his disciples that God—who is far more righteous than this unjust judge—will surely answer the prayers of his people and bring them justice as well. God's people, then, must pray and "not lose heart" (v. 1).

Jesus's second parable illustrates a stark contrast between two different ways to approach God in prayer—one of which we see from a proud
Pharisee and the other from a "sinful" tax collector (18:9–14). The prayer
that the Pharisee offers to God is founded on an arrogant horizontal comparison and involves him thanking God that he is not like the sinners around
him (vv. 11–12). In contrast with this Pharisee's self-exultant prayer, the
tax collector prays humbly for God to show mercy to him, a sinner (v. 13).
Jesus concludes by explaining that the latter's prayer will bring him justi-
fication before God—for humble and repentant sinners will be exalted in
God's sight.

We will not cover Luke 18:15–19:27 in detail either—but please read
through those verses as well. In them, Jesus issues an invitation and call to
have childlike faith, pushes us to abandon the love of money, and issues
clear predictions of his death. He also calls the wealthy and corrupt tax
collector Zacchaeus to himself and then teaches his followers about the
importance of stewarding well the gifts and blessings of God.

Read Luke 17:1–19:27.

GETTING STARTED

1. What have been some of the biggest sources of discouragement to you
regarding your prayer life? What wrong attitudes do you have to battle
as you seek to pray consistently, joyfully, and persistently?

God Gets Us Right, pg. 266–67
The tax collector understood that although there is nothing a sinner
can do to get right with God, God makes sinners right with himself
through the perfect sacrifice of his own blessed Son.

2. Why is comparing ourselves with others (and especially with others whom we perceive to be worse sinners than we are!) so damaging to our understanding of the gospel and the way it is based on Jesus's immense grace for us as sinners?

OBSERVING THE TEXT

3. Note how Luke is careful to include a mention of either the purpose or the audience for both parables that Jesus tells in this passage. How do his narrative comments help us to understand and apply these parables correctly?

4. The concluding words that Jesus delivers after the first parable in this passage help us to connect it in the right way to our prayer lives—as well as to our understanding of the character and promises of our God. What makes the questions that Jesus asks in 18:6–8 powerful and effective?

5. What do the physical postures and demeanors of the two praying men in Jesus's second parable tell us about their attitudes toward God, themselves, and others (18:9–14)?

UNDERSTANDING THE TEXT

6. How does the introduction that Luke gives in 18:1 to Jesus's first parable help us to read and study it, as well as to apply it to our lives in the way that Jesus intends?

7. What does Jesus tell us about the character of the judge in the city where this widow lives (18:2–5)? How does she go about seeking justice—and why does the judge ultimately give in to her requests?

8. As Jesus moves from talking about the unrighteous judge to discussing our righteous Father and his gracious Son (18:6–8), what points does he make about the prayers we offer to God? What encouragement do these verses provide for followers of God?

9. What does 18:9 tell you about the primary audience to whom Jesus addressed his second parable about prayer?

All We Need to Do, pg. 245
Ordinarily we do not get the key to unlock a parable until the end of the story, but this time the key is already in the lock, and all we need to do is open the door. The Son of God—who always prayed to his Father, and who even now prays for us all the time—is telling us not to give up, but to persist in prayer.

10. Notice what the Pharisee's prayer in 18:10–12 emphasizes. What does he seek to call God's attention to—and what does that suggest about the basis of his hope for finding favor with him? What kind of attitudes does his prayer betray that he has toward others?

11. What is strikingly different about the prayer of the tax collector from the prayer of the Pharisee (18:13–14)? What does his prayer reveal about the way that he understands himself as well as the character of God? What encouragement do Jesus's concluding words offer to repentant sinners—and what warning to those who are spiritually proud?

BIBLE CONNECTIONS

12. Read Matthew 7:7–11—a passage from the Sermon on the Mount in which Jesus teaches his disciples about prayer. How is the argument that he makes in Matthew 7 similar to the argument that moves from the lesser to the greater in the first parable from Luke 18?

13. Read Isaiah 66:1–2. How do these verses apply to the second man in Jesus's second parable—and what do they say about the way he will surely be received by God?

THEOLOGY CONNECTIONS

14. Notice that the widow's plea to the unrighteous judge concerns *justice*—and that Jesus promises ultimate justice to God's people at the time of his second coming (Luke 18:8). Why is it important for us to understand that Jesus's parable is *not* teaching us that God will give us whatever we want? What *is* Jesus promising about what God will ultimately do to answer the persistent prayers of his people?

15. The Westminster Shorter Catechism defines repentance in answer 87 as "a saving grace, whereby a sinner, out of a true sense of his sin, and apprehension of the mercy of God in Christ, does, with grief and hatred of his sin, turn from it unto God, with full purpose of, and endeavor after, new obedience." How does the humble prayer that the tax collector offers in the temple show evidence of these attitudes and actions regarding repentance?

APPLYING THE TEXT

16. What evidence do you see that your prayers are not bold, persistent, and faith-filled enough? How can the model of the persistent widow encourage you to pray to your faithful heavenly Father with more earnestness and fervency?

17. What convicts you as you read the self-centered prayer that the Pharisee offers in Jesus's second parable? What reflection do you see in this prayer of the sinful attitudes within your own heart (even if you would never actually *pray* the words that the Pharisee prays)?

18. What should you do to shape your own approach to God to be more like the simple plea of the tax collector—especially regarding the way you pray about the salvation, forgiveness, and pardon you have received? In what way does the tax collector's prayer demonstrate the fundamental hope in the gospel of Jesus Christ that should ground all of our prayers?

PRAYER PROMPT

This passage ought to both expand our confidence and increase our humility as we approach our great and gracious God in prayer! We should have great confidence because our heavenly Father is good and because he hears his children's prayers as their eternally righteous judge. We should have great humility because we come before God as sinners who are trusting alone for saving grace and favor in the mercy that he shows us through his Son. Today, spend some time praying with both confidence and humility as you close this study.

Mercy for the Unrighteous Who Ask, pg. 267

We will never be saved by thinking how righteous we are—as if we were better than anyone else—but only by acknowledging how unrighteous we are. If we want to be saved from sin, we must go to the mercy seat, and there we will receive God's grace, which is available to us today simply for the asking.

LESSON 8

JESUS AND JERUSALEM

Luke 19:28–20:47

THE BIG PICTURE

The passage that you will read in this lesson shows Jesus entering Jerusalem as the day of his betrayal and crucifixion draws near. He rides in on a donkey, to great pomp and praise, as many of the residents of Jerusalem greet him as their Messiah and "King" (19:28–40). As we might expect, the Pharisees are perturbed by the crowds' worship of Jesus (vv. 39–40). We then see Jesus's compassion for the Jewish people, and his longing for them to turn to him in faith, as he weeps while speaking of the unbelief of many in Jerusalem (19:41–44). And he does not only weep—he also cleanses the temple with righteous indignation and drives out the "robbers" who have taken up residence in this place of worship (19:45–46). Then he continues to teach the people, even as the religious leaders also continue to conspire against him (19:47–48).

As the Jewish religious leaders persist in their questioning and challenging of Jesus's authority, he answers their attacks with a question of his own about John the Baptist—a question that is dangerous (to them) and that they cannot answer (20:1–8). Then he tells them a parable to illustrate the truth that, after God's faithful prophets have ministered throughout many generations of the Israelites, the Messiah has now come (20:9–18). This "parable of the wicked tenants" describes how an owner of a vineyard (who represents God and his ownership of Israel) sends servant after servant to collect fruit from the vineyard—only for them to be beaten and sent away empty-handed. Finally the owner of the vineyard sends his own son . . . whom the wicked tenants decide to kill (vv. 13–15). Jesus paints a vivid picture of his own coming: the Messiah will be rejected by many, but those who receive him by faith will be welcomed as children of God.

Please quickly scan through Luke 20:19–47 as well—a section that contains clashes between Jesus and the chief priests, the scribes, and the Sadducees, which take place over issues ranging from taxes to the resurrection to Christ's identity as the son of David.

Read Luke 19:28–20:47.

GETTING STARTED

1. Why do some people embrace *certain* things about Jesus (his teaching, the example he sets, and so on) without believing that he is God or submitting the entirety of their lives to him? How do we know that Jesus has not left this option open to us?

2. What pictures or opinions of Jesus have you seen that emphasize his gentleness to the exclusion of his power, wrath, and judgment? When have you seen others emphasize his judgment and righteousness while neglecting his tenderness and compassion?

Let Your Soul Be Moved, pg. 349

What is your response to this passionate man? Let your heart be touched by the tender compassion he had for lost people in the city. Let your soul be moved by his zeal for the worship of God's house. Let your spirit be captivated by his vision for reaching the whole world with the message of his grace. Surrender your mind to his supreme authority. Hang on to the words of Jesus Christ!

OBSERVING THE TEXT

3. Note the way in which the crowds of people respond to Jesus throughout this passage. How do people other than the Pharisees and scribes respond to him? What is encouraging about their response?

4. How, in contrast, do the religious leaders generally respond to Jesus throughout this passage? What do you note about the replies and reactions that Jesus gives to them in return?

5. Where and how, throughout this passage, does Jesus demonstrate compassion and gentle love? Where and how does he demonstrate anger, zeal, and judgment? What do you learn throughout this text about the heart he has for the people of God?

UNDERSTANDING THE TEXT

6. Read Zechariah 9:9, which provides the prophetic foreshadowing of Jesus's triumphal entry into Jerusalem. How does this prophecy explain the instructions Jesus gives to his disciples in Luke 19:30–31? What is he communicating to his disciples, and to the people of Jerusalem, by riding into the city on a donkey?

7. How do the crowds respond to Jesus in 19:36–38? What does their response indicate about their understanding of his identity? How do the Pharisees react to the crowds—and with what beautiful truth does Jesus confront them in 19:39–40?

8. What does Jesus reveal about the heart he has for lost people—even for those who stubbornly reject him—when he weeps over Jerusalem (19:41–42)? What does he say about Jerusalem's future judgment and destruction—and how does this punishment serve to teach us about the seriousness of sinfully rejecting the Messiah (19:43–44)?

9. What does Luke tell us about Jesus's *motivation* for cleansing the temple (19:45–46)? What does this show us about what Jesus prioritizes in his people—what should they focus on when they are worshiping God?

One of the Clearest Proofs, pg. 336
Jesus refused to be acknowledged as anything except the King! In fact, he said that if people stopped worshiping him, then the whole universe would fill the silence with praise. Jesus could not and would not deny that this is what he truly deserved. Therefore, Palm Sunday is one of the clearest proofs that Jesus really claimed to be the Christ; it shows us for sure that he is our God and our King.

10. Notice the brilliant response that Jesus gives to the chief priests, scribes, and elders when they challenge his authority (20:1–8). Why does his question have the effect of paralyzing them and preventing them from responding—and what does it reveal about the way they have rejected God and his servants?

11. Jesus's parable serves as an overview of the Old Testament history that led up to his arrival as God's Son—the Messiah (20:9–18). Who do the characters in the parable represent? What stern warning does Jesus offer about the way we respond to him (20:17–18)?

BIBLE CONNECTIONS

12. Read Zechariah 9:10–13 and take note of the promises God makes to his people in these verses that follow 9:9, which we have already read. What will happen for God's people when his chosen King comes? What will characterize this Messiah's rule?

13. Read Isaiah 56:6–8. What is Jesus communicating to the Jews by quoting from verse 7 of this text while he is in the midst of cleansing the temple in Jerusalem (Luke 19:46)?

THEOLOGY CONNECTIONS

14. To explain how Jesus Christ acts as our King, answer 26 of the Westminster Shorter Catechism says that "Christ executes the office of a king, in subduing us to himself, in ruling and defending us, and in restraining and conquering all his and our enemies." How does Jesus's triumphal entry highlight the role that he holds as King—and what makes his kingship into a source of eternal encouragement for his people?

15. Jesus offers this passage's harshest words of warning at the conclusion of his parable, when he cautions the religious leaders lest the Son of God, whom they are rejecting, "crush" them (20:18). What does this warning indicate about what lies ahead for people who reject Jesus Christ? What role does the doctrine of the exclusivity of Jesus Christ play in this warning?

APPLYING THE TEXT

16. How should the way in which Jesus was exalted and worshiped as he rode into Jerusalem motivate our worship and adoration of him? What keeps you from exultantly worshiping your Savior? What can God's people do to encourage and prompt one another to praise him the way that he deserves?

17. What do you find convicting about Jesus's zealous and angry cleansing of the temple in Jerusalem? What does this account reveal about Jesus's passionate commitment to the pure worship of God—as well as about his anger over people's corruption, greed, and selfish distraction of others from their worship?

18. How can this passage drive you to evangelize and witness for the gospel boldly? In what way should the account of Jesus's weeping over Jerusalem shape your heart's disposition regarding those who do not yet know him as Savior and Lord?

PRAYER PROMPT

This passage has confronted us with a grand vision of the future rule and judgment of Jesus Christ along with describing the compassion that he feels. As you conclude this study, pray first that God would enable you to bow before him and offer him true and humble worship, adoration, and praise! Then ask him, by his Spirit, to give you a heart that is compassionate and is zealous for him—one that is patterned after your Savior. Pray to be able to weep for those who do not know him, and ask God to make you passionately committed to offering holy and reverent worship to Jesus in all that you do.

The Cornerstone, pg. 361

Jesus said it himself: he is the precious stone that God has chosen to be the cornerstone of the church. But if we trip over him, he will fall on us with crushing force. This is why Jesus was weeping when he rode into Jerusalem. He knew what would happen to people who rejected him as the Only Beloved Son.

LESSON 9

THE FINAL JUDGMENT

Luke 21:1–38

THE BIG PICTURE

In the passage we will study for this lesson, Jesus directs his disciples to consider the days to come—both the days of trouble and destruction that await the city of Jerusalem and its temple as well as the ultimate day of judgment that awaits the entire world. Even though the instructions he gives regarding these days are weighty and full of warning, they also demonstrate his love for his disciples—which includes those who follow him today! Our Savior wants us to live as his obedient, faithful, and expectant witnesses in light of his return.

After briefly highlighting the generous heart that a poor widow displays (21:1–4), Luke focuses on a particular conversation that Jesus has with his disciples, which begins as the disciples are admiring the beauty of the temple in Jerusalem (21:5). Jesus responds by describing a day when this beautiful temple will be destroyed—a day that will take place during a time of great tumult, violence, and spiritual deception (21:6–9). He goes on to describe the terrible persecution that his followers will experience in the days ahead, which will be times of war, political oppression, and violence against God's people that they will need to faithfully endure (21:10–19). He then returns to the theme of the eventual destruction and fall that is to come to Jerusalem when a great Gentile army will invade and conquer it in addition to putting many to the sword (21:20–24).

Then, in 21:25–38, Jesus directs his disciples' gaze farther into the future—to the day of his second coming. The "Son of Man" will come with power and will institute a great day of redemption for God's people (vv. 25–28). He says that his disciples should look for the signs of his coming, which will be as evident as the way the leaves on a fig tree point to the coming summer (vv. 29–33). Jesus's teaching ends with a final word of warning for his disciples: they must stay awake and undistracted and always remain ready for his return and for the day when all people will stand before him to be judged (vv. 34–36).

Read Luke 21:1–38.

GETTING STARTED

1. How have you seen the end of the world portrayed in films, novels, or other forms of entertainment or art? What do these portrayals reveal about what most people think concerning the final days of the world—if they think about them at all?

2. What makes it difficult for us to seriously consider the second coming of Jesus Christ during our day-to-day lives? Has the reality of the final judgment sometimes seemed unreal to you? Why or why not?

Are You Ready for the End of the World? pg. 442
We cannot simply drift through life without thinking seriously about the end of the world. The decision we make about Jesus Christ now determines where we will end up for all eternity. This is a matter of spiritual life and death. . . . Are you ready for the end of the world?

OBSERVING THE TEXT

3. The conversation that Jesus's disciples have in Luke 21:5 about the temple seems to be the launching point for Jesus's teaching about the destruction of Jerusalem and the final judgment of the world. Why do you think Jesus chooses to make this connection? What does this tell you about the tone of the disciples' conversation?

4. Consult a reference Bible or Philip Ryken's commentary on Luke for more context regarding the events that are prophesied throughout Luke 21:5–24. What seems to be the timeframe for the events that Jesus foretells in this passage?

5. What signals for us, in 21:25–38, that Jesus is shifting his gaze farther into the future and describing the end of the world?

UNDERSTANDING THE TEXT

6. What does Jesus prophesy about the temple as his disciples are admiring it (21:5–9)? What warnings does he offer in these verses as he tells them about the coming destruction?

7. What does Jesus say to his disciples about the conflict and political tension that will take place in the days to come (21:10–12)? What will these days hold in store for his followers—and what opportunities will they have, even in the midst of what happens to them (21:13–19)?

8. What does Jesus say lies ahead for the city of Jerusalem (21:20–24)? Who will conquer the city—and what does verse 22 say is the ultimate reason for this defeat that Jerusalem will experience? How does this prophecy demonstrate God's character and the perspective he takes on sin and rebellion that is committed against him—especially by people who have heard his call and rejected it?

9. As Jesus looks farther into the future and describes the second coming of the Son of Man, what picture does he paint of his return (21:25–27)? What will cause this to be a frightening day for Jesus's enemies and a glorious day for his people? What does 21:28 tell us about the hope God's people should have as they look toward the day of Christ's return?

Four Practical Exhortations, pg. 413

To help us know how to live from now until the end of the world, Jesus gives four practical exhortations that we can list as a series of "don'ts": don't be led astray; don't be afraid; don't miss the opportunity to witness; and don't give up.

10. Look at what Jesus says in 21:29–31 about the fig tree. What point is he making to his disciples through this comparison regarding the fig tree, its leaves, and what it indicates about summer? How does knowing about the day of Christ's return and about the final judgment remind us of our need to cling to God's Word as our authority and guide (21:32–33)?

11. What additional warnings does Jesus offer to his disciples in 21:34–36 regarding the way they should await his second coming? What do his instructions say about the way his followers ought to live in the meantime?

BIBLE CONNECTIONS

12. Although Jesus's disciples may have been horrified by his prophecy about the temple's destruction, Jesus had already explained that *he* himself was the fulfillment of the temple—the ultimate meeting place between a holy God and a sinful people. Read John 2:19–22 and note what Jesus says about the temple of his body. What does John tell us in verse 22 about the understanding that came to his disciples after his death and resurrection?

13. Read 2 Peter 3:8–10. What does the apostle Peter say is God's reason for delaying the day of judgment? What additional descriptions does Peter offer about the day of the Lord that will ultimately come?

THEOLOGY CONNECTIONS

14. What Jesus said about the fall of Jerusalem and the destruction of the temple came to pass in A.D. 70, when the Romans put down a Judean revolt that led to a lengthy siege of the city. In what way could these events be seen as a day of "vengeance" such as God's Word described? Why isn't the destruction of the physical temple in Jerusalem detrimental to God's grand plan of redemption (see question 12)?

15. The Westminster Confession of Faith has this to say about the day of judgment: "The end of God's appointing this day is for the manifestation of the glory of his mercy in the eternal salvation of the elect, and of his justice in the damnation of the reprobate" (33.2). In what ways has the passage that we have been studying described both the mercy and the justice of God that will accompany the return of Jesus Christ?

APPLYING THE TEXT

16. How should the reminder that Jesus gives to the disciples—that even the grand temple in Jerusalem is temporary—serve to shape our perspective on the seemingly strong and sturdy things of this world? What things that you tend to see as being permanent can this passage help to remind you are actually temporary?

17. What warnings does Jesus issue in this passage regarding *deception*—and how should we apply those warnings as we see and hear the predictions and teaching that take place in the world around us today?

18. What things most often distract you from thinking about Jesus's second coming? What habits and practices could you adopt that would awaken you more regularly to the reality of the final judgment—and how could this help to encourage your faith and strengthen your obedience and witness?

Don't Miss Jesus, pg. 444

What is the temptation for you? Are you finding comfort in the drunken pleasures of a fallen world? If so, you are only hurting yourself, and the people you love. But maybe you are driving yourself to distraction with all the things you are doing, including all the things you think you are doing for God. Be careful, or else you will miss Jesus on the last day and come under judgment.

PRAYER PROMPT

This passage is full of grave warning—but also full of hope for those who know and love Jesus Christ. This world is *not* our final home or our final hope; Jesus, our King, *will* return. Today, as you close your study of this section of Luke's gospel, pray for God to give you the strength to live a life that is *ready* for the return of Jesus Christ. Ask for his help with being vigilant and obedient, guarded against deception, and ready at all times to bear witness to the gospel. Pray to be able to look for the return of your Savior hopefully and expectantly!

LESSON 10

THE LAST SUPPER

Luke 22:1–46

THE BIG PICTURE

The opening of Luke 22 makes it evident that the plot against Jesus's life is thickening . . . and is, in fact, about to be set in motion. The chief priests and scribes are continuing to connive against him (22:1–2)—and on top of that, now Judas, one of Jesus's own disciples, gives in to temptation from Satan and joins the plot against Jesus's life (22:3–6).

As this chapter goes on, it helps us to see the servant heart of the Savior who will go to the cross on behalf of sinners—and all according to the perfect will of his Father in heaven. Jesus leads his disciples to prepare for the Passover meal (22:7–13) and reclines at table with them for a final supper before his death. He institutes the Lord's Supper and declares that his body and his blood now institute a "new covenant" of God's forgiveness that will be made available through his perfect and final sacrifice for sinners (22:14–20). As he does so, Jesus also alludes to his imminent betrayal by one of his own disciples (22:21–23).

As an unseemly debate breaks out among the disciples about which of them is the greatest (22:24), Jesus explains yet again what constitutes true greatness in his kingdom: loving service (22:25–30). The ultimate example of this service will occur at the cross. He goes on to predict Peter's denial before insisting that the Scripture must be fulfilled that says the Messiah will be numbered with "transgressors"—indeed, Jesus's death will atone for even disciples like Peter who falter in their faith and temporarily deny him (22:31–38).

The end of this passage takes us to the scene of Jesus's prayer near the Mount of Olives, during which he struggles with the reality of the suffering that lies ahead of him—before ultimately committing himself to the perfect will of his Father (22:39–46). The Messiah will now march to the sacrificial death that he will endure in the place of sinners, according to the perfect and eternal plan of God.

Read Luke 22:1–46.

GETTING STARTED

1. Describe times you have seen Jesus being portrayed as an unwilling, helpless victim. How does this view lead to misunderstandings about his death—and what damage can this cause to the message of the gospel?

2. What have you found encouraging, in your study of Luke thus far, regarding the way Jesus's disciples have been responding to his leadership and teaching? What have you been disappointed by? How might you have reacted if Jesus had predicted that *you* would deny and abandon him in his moment of greatest need, as he has predicted that Peter will?

Jesus Is Praying for Us, pg. 491–92

If only we could see Jesus on his knees and listen to what he is saying to the Father, what courage we would take to live for him through every trouble in life. Jesus is praying for us, that our faith will not fail. . . . He is praying about our wandering into sin, that we will never stop trusting in his forgiveness. Jesus is praying for everything we need.

OBSERVING THE TEXT

3. Note the different ways in which people respond to Jesus throughout this passage. How do the religious leaders respond to him? What are his disciples distracted by—and what do they still not understand about Jesus's purpose and his kingdom?

4. What truths is Jesus seeking to teach his disciples throughout this passage—and how do these truths contrast with many of our natural tendencies and assumptions?

5. In what places throughout this passage do you see Jesus's own understanding of the purpose for his death being made evident?

UNDERSTANDING THE TEXT

6. What can we assume is at least *part* of the motivation Judas had for betraying Jesus, based on what we read in Luke 22:3–6? What involvement does Luke indicate that Satan himself had in this unthinkable betrayal?

7. What does Jesus teach the disciples about the meaning of his death as he institutes the "Lord's Supper" in 22:14–20? What is the significance of the fact that he institutes this meal during the feast of the Passover (what connection does he want his disciples to make)?

8. What is so surprising about the debate that arises among Jesus's disciples during the Passover meal (22:24)? What does Jesus say characterizes true greatness in his kingdom (22:25–30)? How will the actions that he is soon to take provide the ultimate example of true greatness?

9. What does Peter say in an attempt to defend his strength and his undying loyalty to Jesus (22:31–34)? What gracious promises does Jesus make in conjunction with his prediction about Peter's failure?

10. Notice the instructions Jesus gives to his disciples in 22:35–38. What do the details of what he says imply about the times that lie ahead for his followers? In what way do his words in verse 37 again illustrate the purpose of his impending death on the cross?

A Life of Service, pg. 482
Jesus had been serving his disciples since the day they started to follow him—leading them, feeding them, healing them, teaching them, correcting them, training them, and loving them. Soon he would serve them all the way to the death, bearing their sins all the way to the grave.

11. What does the agony that Jesus displays during his prayer tell us about the pain and wrath he is about to face (22:39–46)? How does he ultimately demonstrate submission to the will of God? What do you notice about the disciples' behavior as their Savior is in the midst of this earnest prayer and struggle?

BIBLE CONNECTIONS

12. Read John 12:1–8, and notice the insight that John gives us in verse 6 regarding Judas's disordered loves and greedy motivations. How does John's insight help us to understand the avenue that Satan used to grip Judas's heart and turn him against the very Son of God, whom he had been following for three years?

13. During the first Passover, the angel of the Lord, as he was bringing judgment on the people of Egypt, passed over the homes of God's people who had marked their doors with blood from a lamb. With this story in mind, read 1 Corinthians 5:7. What explicit connection does Paul make between Jesus's death and the Passover? How does the crucifixion serve as the Passover's ultimate fulfillment?

THEOLOGY CONNECTIONS

14. The Westminster Confession of Faith explains that God's "covenant of grace" was "differently administered in the time of the law, and in the time of the gospel; under the law it was administered by promises, prophecies, sacrifices, circumcision, the paschal lamb, and other types and ordinances delivered to the people of the Jews, all foresignifying Christ to come" (7.5). How does this description of the covenant help to explain what Jesus is saying in Luke 22:20 about his blood?

15. In Luke 22:21–23, Jesus makes plain the reality that God's sovereign purposes and human responsibility coexist together. What does he say about the role that God's purpose plays in his death? How does he speak to Judas's guilt and the punishment he will receive for his actions?

APPLYING THE TEXT

16. What warning does the story of Judas offer to us? What idolatrous loves may be tugging at your heart and tempting you away from clinging faithfully, devotedly, and worshipfully to Jesus?

17. Did anything strike you in a fresh way about this passage's depiction of the institution of the Lord's Supper? If so, how can this enhance the way you understand your own participation in this sacred meal?

What must we celebrate, and how must we worship, when we receive Communion with God's people?

18. What example does Jesus provide of the way we should pray and the attitude we should hold toward our heavenly Father when he surrenders his will to the Father's will—even when it means he will journey to the cross? What specific desires might need to change in your heart as you submit to the will of God more humbly and fully?

PRAYER PROMPT

This passage confronts us with the steadfast faithfulness, service, humility, and perfect obedience of our Savior—all of which stands in contrast to the betrayal, weakness, and lack of understanding that we see in his disciples. Judas betrays Jesus and comes against him with violence—and even Peter is predicted to deny his Lord during his moment of greatest vulnerability! This is a passage that of necessity drives us to our knees to worship, adore, repent before, and place our faith in our Savior. Praise God for his eternal and perfect plan to redeem us through his Son. And praise the Son for choosing to be numbered with "transgressors" in order to save your sinful soul.

Surrendered Will, pg. 508

Now Jesus empowers us to follow his example in surrendering our own will to the will of God. It is not wrong to tell God what we truly desire, but even the good things we want must always be surrendered to the superior wisdom of his fatherly will. "Thy will be done" is one of the main petitions in the daily prayer that Jesus taught us to pray (see Matt. 6:10). Thus our Lord calls us to pray this way through all the hard situations in life.

LESSON 11

THE TRIALS

Luke 22:47–23:25

THE BIG PICTURE

Our passage for this lesson begins with Jesus being betrayed by one of his own, continues as we see Peter's painful denial of him, and then goes on to show us several unjust trials and examinations by political leaders. Jesus, the innocent Son of God, is betrayed by his own followers and unjustly condemned to death by sinful men who have selfish agendas. Yet the Messiah is no helpless, unwilling victim! Jesus calmly endures betrayal, denial, injustice, and ultimately death—all for the sake of redeeming God's people who will put their faith in him.

After Judas leads the servants of the high priest to Jesus in order to arrest him (22:47–53), Peter follows this band of men to the high priest's house, where they have taken Jesus to begin his "trial" (22:54–62). Upon being questioned three different times regarding his connection to Jesus, Peter denies even knowing him—just as Jesus had predicted (v. 60). Jesus, meanwhile, endures mistreatment, beatings, and merciless mockery at the hands of the chief priest's men (22:63–65).

Then the so-called trials of Jesus begin—trials that are full of corruption, false accusations, and outright lies. The Jewish council accuses Jesus of blasphemy when he bears faithful witness to his identity after being asked if he is the Son of God (22:66–71). They send him to Pilate, the Roman governor of the region, who finds no guilt in Jesus that would cause him to deserve death and declares him innocent (23:1–5). Jesus is then sent from

Pilate to Herod, the Roman-appointed "King of the Jews," who questions and mocks Jesus before sending him back to Pilate (23:6–12). Once he is before Pilate again, Jesus finally is sentenced to death as the murderous Jewish leaders convince Pilate to release a violent criminal in his place and to sentence Jesus to death by crucifixion (23:13–25).

Read Luke 22:47–23:25.

GETTING STARTED

1. Most of us imagine that we would choose to do the right thing even if we were in a moment of danger and risk—would choose, for instance, to stand by a friend or make a costly sacrifice. What hints have we seen in our study of Luke thus far that this is *not* what Jesus's disciples will choose—that instead he will be abandoned by even his closest friends and will ultimately go the cross alone?

2. What disturbs us so much about injustice—especially when we see it happening at the highest levels of law, politics, and rule? Why are we wired to desire justice—and to hate, for instance, when an innocent victim is murdered?

OBSERVING THE TEXT

3. What examples of obvious injustice do you see throughout this passage? How does Luke make it evident to his readers that Jesus is completely faultless and innocent?

4. What signs do you see, as you read and study this passage, that Jesus is in complete control throughout what happens in it? How does it show us that Jesus is not a helpless, unwilling victim but is instead going willingly and faithfully to his sacrificial death?

5. In what ways do Jesus's disciples fail him throughout this passage? How does Luke make it clear that Jesus is standing *alone* as the perfectly faithful one who will die for sinners—which, as the passage proves, includes his own disciples?

Innocent, pg. 555

Jesus was innocent of all these charges. Indeed, he was innocent of any charge that anyone could bring against him. He was and is the only perfectly innocent man who ever lived. This was so obvious that even Pontius Pilate managed to recognize it and reach the right verdict, at which point the case should have been closed. . . . But the whole ghastly affair did not stop there. It kept right on going until the King of the Jews was dying, bleeding on the cross in naked innocence.

UNDERSTANDING THE TEXT

6. As Judas leads the chief priest's men to arrest Jesus, how do Jesus's
   disciples initially respond to what is happening (22:49–50)? What do
   you notice about the statements Jesus makes in this opening section
   of the passage (22:47–53)? What do his words demonstrate about his
   understanding of the situation—and how do they convey his complete
   calmness and control?

7. What seems to motivate Peter to deny Jesus when he is in the courtyard
   of the chief priest (22:54–62)? What risks would he have embraced if
   he had boldly announced his connection with Jesus? How can we tell
   that the Spirit immediately convicts Peter of his sinful denial as Jesus
   turns to look at him (23:61–62)?

8. How do the servants of the chief priest treat Jesus—and what does
   this treatment imply about the understanding they have regarding his
   identity and the claims he has made (22:63–64)? What makes the
   "testimony" that Jesus offers about his identity so offensive and worthy
   of punishment, from the perspective of the elders (22:66–71)? Why
   would we ourselves label the claim that he makes as blasphemy . . . if
   it were made by anyone else?

9. What do you find striking about the initial interaction between Pilate and Jesus, which occurs in 23:1–5? What truth does Pilate affirm about the Son of God—and what does Luke portray even this pagan ruler demonstrating regarding Jesus's innocence?

10. Notice the unlikely friendship that forms between Pilate and Herod as they pass Jesus back and forth between each other (23:12). What is ironic about this development? What do both men seem to conclude about Jesus, as a result of their examinations of him, before they send him back to the Jewish leaders (23:6–16)?

11. What ultimately leads to the death and crucifixion of Jesus—and what group of people most fervently push for his death (23:17–25)? Why does Pilate ultimately give in to the will of the Jewish leaders—and what might be his motivation for doing so?

We Must Pray for Courage, pg. 528

Peter failed that test. This was partly because he was so proudly confident of his faithful discipleship that he did not even pray for God's help. How vulnerable we are to social pressure when we do not ask God to make us as courageous for Christ as we say we want to be when we are alone with Jesus.

BIBLE CONNECTIONS

12. Read Isaiah 53:4–9, and note the specific things this prophecy says about the innocent and suffering Messiah who would be cruelly and unjustly treated. How does this prophecy capture the way Jesus is treated in this passage we are studying?

13. In 1 Peter 2:19–24, Peter uses the suffering that Jesus endured at the hands of unjust men as an example of how we, as his followers, are to faithfully endure unjust treatment of our own. Read those verses now and restate, in your own words, what we are to do when we are treated unfairly.

THEOLOGY CONNECTIONS

14. Answer 49 of the Westminster Larger Catechism tells us that "Christ humbled himself in his death, in that having been betrayed by Judas, forsaken by his disciples, scorned and rejected by the world, condemned by Pilate, and tormented by his persecutors; having also conflicted with the terrors of death, and the powers of darkness, [he] felt . . . the weight of God's wrath." Why is it important for our understanding of Jesus's suffering and humiliation to encapsulate the betrayal, denial, and mockery that he endured along with his death?

15. The complete fallenness, sinfulness, and spiritual deadness that the doctrine of *total depravity* teaches us about is on full display in this passage from Luke. In what way does the account of Jesus's trial highlight humanity's evil? What do the accounts of his betrayal and Peter's denial highlight about the weakness and need that characterize even the friends of Jesus?

APPLYING THE TEXT

16. How should Judas's betrayal, and Peter's denial, of Jesus serve to warn us, convict us, and guide us to boldly and courageously commit to and witness for him? When are you most tempted to deny Jesus? What can you do, now, to prepare to stand boldly for him—even when doing so may be costly?

God Works in the Darkness, pg. 520

What comfort and courage this gives to us in every dark hour. It is true that our present trials will not last forever. Soon we will enter the eternal light of our salvation. But even this present darkness—whatever it is for us—is under the power of God. If God was at work even during the dark hour of our Lord's betrayal, then whether we can see it or not, we may believe with hope that he is also at work right now in our own dark trials.

17. In what ways does this passage serve to increase your love, adoration, and worship of Jesus your Savior as well as your gratitude to him? What struck you anew, as you read the passage, about all that he endured, suffered, and willingly bore so that he could go to the cross to die for *your* sins?

18. What does the fact that God's plan and purpose were at work even in the ugly betrayal and unjust trial that Jesus experienced tell you about the loving control he has over even trials, suffering, and cruel injustice? What do you need to remember today about the eternally good purposes God has—even (and especially) for your pain? How can the reality of these good purposes encourage you?

PRAYER PROMPT

This passage confronts us with the absolute innocence, perfection, and holiness of Jesus Christ, the Son of God—along with his willingness to face the cruelty and suffering that lay ahead of him. In his final hours, Jesus is left completely alone—he is betrayed by Judas, denied by Peter, hated by the Jewish leaders, and abandoned by Pilate and Herod, who could have insisted that he be treated justly. Horrific injustice abounds during Jesus's final hours—and yet the perfect Savior goes willingly toward the cross, in accordance with the perfect plan of the Father. Conclude this lesson by praising, thanking, and showing gratitude to your Savior, who endured all this for your eternal salvation!

LESSON 12

JESUS'S DEATH AND BURIAL

Luke 23:26–56

THE BIG PICTURE

In this passage, Luke records for his readers the darkest day in all of history: the crucifixion of the Lord Jesus Christ—the Son of God. The Messiah is finally led to his crucifixion, carrying his own cross and being mocked mercilessly along the way. Yet even as he is at the apex of his suffering, we receive a glimpse of the glorious salvation that will come as a result of this darkest day, as Jesus promises forgiveness and life to a criminal who has been crucified beside him! The day of great darkness will, according to the plan of God, be the day of bright salvation for sinners.

As Jesus is led away to be crucified, a man named Simon of Cyrene is recruited to help with carrying his cross—most likely because Jesus is exhausted and near the point of collapse (23:26). While he is walking, Jesus again describes the day of trouble—and weeping—that is coming for the city of Jerusalem (23:27–31). Then, on a cross that is marked "King of the Jews," Jesus is mocked and derided—even as he graciously prays for the forgiveness of those who are murdering him (23:32–38). Luke alone records the moment during Jesus's crucifixion when, as one of the criminals who has been crucified next to Jesus mocks him bitterly, the criminal on his other side pleads in faith for Jesus to remember him when he comes into his kingdom (23:39–43). This criminal then receives the promise of eternal salvation from the crucified Savior.

At the precise moment of Jesus's death, great darkness descends upon the land—and the curtain of the temple is torn in two (23:44–45). Jesus commits his soul to God the Father as a Roman centurion who is watching him declares his innocence (23:46–49). Jesus, who is truly physically dead, is then buried in the tomb of a man named Joseph as the Sabbath rest begins (23:50–56). The Messiah has been crucified for the sins of God's people; now he waits in the tomb for the moment of resurrection.

Read Luke 23:26–56.

GETTING STARTED

1. Many people in our world today have some measure of respect for Jesus—at least as a model, a teacher, or a great example. What are people missing when their understanding of Jesus leaves out the reality, and the meaning, of his death on the cross?

2. Why do stories of martyrs inspire us? What amazes us about someone who sacrifices his or her life for a greater purpose? Why, however, is it important for us to see Jesus's death as being infinitely more significant than the death of any other martyr in history?

The Cross, pg. 570–71

The whole Gospel of Luke has been leading to this point—the point where we see the cross. Luke is "the Gospel of knowing for sure" (see Luke 1:1–4), and for a long time we have known for sure that Jesus would have to die. . . . But here, finally, Luke shows us the cross.

OBSERVING THE TEXT

3. What glimpses do you see throughout this passage of the way Jesus understands the purpose of his death? How does he demonstrate his gracious saving purposes even while he is enduring excruciating pain and suffering?

4. What do you notice about the way the people who are surrounding Jesus react to him as he dies? What examples of anger and mockery do you see from some of them? How do others demonstrate surprising faith and admiration?

5. How does Luke remind us of Jesus' true *identity* throughout this passage—both through his narration and even through the mockery we see from Jesus's enemies?

UNDERSTANDING THE TEXT

6. What do the words Jesus says to the weeping "daughters of Jerusalem" illustrate, again, about the times of suffering that are to come for God's people (23:27–31)?

7. What does the response that Jesus gives to his enemies and persecutors show us about his heart (23:32–34)? What hope does the prayer that he offers from the cross give to sinners who repent and turn in faith to him?

8. What do you think was the intention behind the inscription reading "King of the Jews" that was placed on Jesus's cross (23:35–38)? What purpose did God have for it being placed there?

9. What is surprising about the interaction Jesus has with the two criminals who are crucified with him (23:39–43)? How does he respond to the man who humbly asks Jesus to "remember" him in his kingdom? What does this teach us about the gospel of grace?

A Sign from the Father, pg. 586

The handwriting on the cross is a sign that no one should miss because it was put there by the love of God. The sign was there because God loves his Son. Even when Jesus was battered and bruised, dying in the guilt of our sin and therefore forsaken, the Father God declared his kingship, making a royal announcement to the world: "This is the King of the Jews." . . . God was saying with fatherly affection, "My Son is the King!"

10. Notice the details surrounding Jesus's death that Luke includes in
    23:44–45—and particularly the darkness and the tearing of the temple
    curtain. What is God communicating through this descending dark-
    ness? What does the torn temple curtain teach us about the significance
    of Jesus's death? What does the centurion's cry further explain about
    the meaning of the cross (23:47)?

11. What details does Luke include in the final section of this passage in
    order to demonstrate that Jesus has really, truly, physically died (23:50–
    56)? What emotions are his readers meant to feel as the passage ends?
    What have Jesus's words led Luke's audience to anticipate will happen
    soon?

BIBLE CONNECTIONS

12. Skim through Leviticus 16 before reading verses 29–34 closely. This
    chapter describes the "Day of Atonement" on which the high priest
    would enter into the holy of holies in order to make sacrifices for the
    sins of God's people. How does this Old Testament chapter inform your
    understanding of the purpose of the curtain that was in the temple and
    the reason that it was torn in two at the moment of Jesus's death?

13. Read 1 Corinthians 15:1–4 and note how Paul includes Jesus's death and burial in his list of things that are of "first importance" to his proclamation of the gospel. Why is it crucial to our belief of the gospel, and to our attempts to explain it to others, for us to affirm that Jesus really, physically died and was buried?

THEOLOGY CONNECTIONS

14. We know that Jesus's death was unlike any other death in history because of the significance it had for the salvation of God's people. The Westminster Confession of Faith explains it this way: "The Lord Jesus, by his perfect obedience and sacrifice of himself, which he through the eternal Spirit once offered up unto God, has fully satisfied the justice of his Father; and purchased not only reconciliation, but an everlasting inheritance in the kingdom of heaven, for all those whom the Father has given unto him" (8.5). What does this explanation tell us that Jesus accomplished through the cross—and what aspects of it are particularly encouraging to you?

15. How does the tearing of the temple curtain vividly illustrate the significance that Jesus's death has to our salvation? What does the conversation that he has with the thief on the cross teach us about salvation—about what God does, and what is required of us, within that process?

APPLYING THE TEXT

16. How does this passage force us to confront our own sin and rebellion against God—along with the reality that we, as a result, played a role in the crucifixion of Jesus Christ? Why must the first way that we apply this text to our lives be to recognize ourselves among Jesus's enemies?

17. What should cause the prayer that Jesus offers from the cross in 23:34 to be deeply encouraging to us, whose sin makes us his natural enemies?

18. How can the conversion of the criminal who is crucified with Jesus serve to strengthen our faith in Jesus's saving power (23:43)? How can it encourage our gospel witness and evangelism?

Saved Forever, pg. 601

Jesus will not forget. Anyone who prays to him in repentance and faith will be saved forever. Jesus said this in the strongest possible terms, as he promised the reward of a gracious Savior: "Truly, I say to you, today you will be with me in Paradise" (Luke 23:43). "Yes," Jesus was saying, "I will not forget; I will remember you." But he was also giving the convert on the cross far more than he asked or imagined.

PRAYER PROMPT

Even during Jesus's moments of greatest suffering and agony, his identity and saving purposes are perfectly clear. The "King of the Jews" gives his life to bring about the forgiveness of sinners who stand in need of God's mercy—and he even demonstrates this saving purpose as he dies by welcoming a repentant criminal into God's eternal kingdom by giving him a gracious promise. Today, praise Jesus for the suffering he willingly endured in your place. Thank him for the prayer of forgiveness that he offered from the cross—a prayer that he offered on your behalf as well as the behalf of every child of God. Ask God for joy and courage to be able to spread the good news of your merciful Savior to sinners who need him.

LESSON 13

THE FIRST EASTER

Luke 24:1–53

THE BIG PICTURE

In our last lesson, we focused on Jesus's sacrificial death and saw God's saving purposes at work even during the darkest day of history. But Jesus's death is not the end of the gospel story; the efficacy of his sacrifice and his triumph over sin and death would not have been confirmed without his glorious resurrection. In the passage for today, we will consider the interactions and teaching that take place upon Jesus's bodily resurrection—the event that clinches his saving work and guarantees the final glorious resurrection of all who repent and put their faith in him.

Luke 24 begins as a group of women visit the tomb of Jesus with spices for his buried body—only to discover that Jesus is gone (24:1–3). They are confronted by two angelic visitors who remind them what Jesus had said about his resurrection. The women report what they have seen and heard to Jesus's disciples, who struggle at first with disbelief (24:4–12). The first glimpse that we get of the resurrected Christ is on the road to Emmaus, in a beautiful account (that Luke alone records) of a conversation that Jesus has with two disciples who are from his broader group of followers (24:13–35). He explains to the distraught pair how his entire life, death, and resurrection have taken place in accordance with the Old Testament Scriptures—and then, just as they begin to recognize him, he vanishes!

Finally Jesus appears to all his disciples as they are gathered together; he speaks words of peace to them, eats with them, and allows them to touch his physical, resurrected body (24:36–43). He goes on to explain how Scripture has been fulfilled through his resurrection and then commands them to wait in the city until they are powerfully clothed with God's Spirit (24:44–49). Jesus ultimately leads his disciples to Bethany, where he ascends to heaven and leaves them worshiping him and rejoicing in the gospel hope that they will soon proclaim to the world (24:50–53).

Read Luke 24:1–53.

GETTING STARTED

1. Many people today consider Jesus's resurrection, along with the hope of eternal life in heaven, to be a religious myth or fairy tale. Why might this be? What compelling explanation could you offer to a skeptic of the reasonableness of believing in the resurrection?

2. What spiritual dangers could result from talking *only* about the cross of Jesus and never talking or thinking deeply about the meaning and significance of his resurrection?

We Will Rise Again, pg. 676

We . . . will go down to the grave. But through faith in Jesus, and by the power of his resurrection, we will rise again. We will see the glory on the other side, and we will rise with Jesus on the final day. Do not disbelieve in the resurrection of the body, but believe it . . . for joy!

OBSERVING THE TEXT

3. What do you notice about the ways that Jesus's followers *initially* respond to the news they receive about his resurrection throughout this passage? Why do you think they are responding in these ways at first?

4. What happens to the women at the tomb, the disciples who are on the road to Emmaus, and the disciples who are gathered together as they come to accept the reality of Jesus's resurrection? What role does God's Word, which includes Jesus's own promises, play in bringing them to a place of belief, faith, and confidence?

5. How do the purposes that Jesus describes for his disciples, as he prepares for his ascension, illustrate an outward movement that incorporates mission, witness, and proclamation? What do we learn about the role these disciples will play in the world in response to what Jesus has just accomplished through his death and resurrection?

UNDERSTANDING THE TEXT

6. As Luke begins his account of the resurrection, in 24:1–7, why do you think he chooses to lead with Jesus's *absence* and with the words that the angels speak to the women who are at his tomb? What do the angels remind the women of?

7. What effect does Luke imply that the words of the angel have on the women (24:8)? How do the disciples respond to the women's report— and what makes this disappointing (24:9–12)?

8. What is Luke's description of the demeanor of the two disciples who meet Jesus on the road to Emmaus—and what does Jesus do to gently rebuke and confront them (24:13–27)? What is the content of the "sermon" that Jesus preaches to them as they walk? What does that sermon teach us about the Old Testament and the unity of all the Scriptures?

Walking on the Gospel Road, pg. 642–43

There [are many] famous events from the life of Christ that people wish they could see: the shepherds at the manger, the baptism in the Jordan . . . or his glorious transfiguration on the mountain. . . . But I would choose to travel the gospel road from Jerusalem to Emmaus, walking with two disciples on an Easter afternoon and listening to Jesus explain how everything in the whole Bible is all about him.

9. How do the two disciples respond to the fellowship and teaching that Jesus has shared with them (24:28–32)? How do they describe this experience to Jesus's disciples—and what is evident about their faith, and their understanding of the event, as they do so (24:33–35)?

10. Notice the actions that Jesus performs when he finally appears to his disciples (24:36–43). In what way do they demonstrate to us that his resurrection body is real? What hints does this passage give us regarding the resurrected bodies that will be ours in the new heaven and new earth during the days to come?

11. What connections does Jesus draw from his death and resurrection to the Old Testament Scriptures—and what finally begins to happen in the disciples' minds and hearts (24:44–46)? How does Jesus call his disciples to respond to his saving work after he has departed (24:47–49)? After he ascends into heaven, what signs do we see that the disciples are ready to proclaim the gospel (24:50–53)?

BIBLE CONNECTIONS

12. In the previous lesson, we began reading 1 Corinthians 15. Return to that passage, this time reading verses 1–8, and note the way Paul explains the gospel of "first importance" that he preached. Why do you think he takes up so much of these verses emphasizing not only Jesus's resurrection but also all the post-resurrection *appearances* he made to his various disciples and to others? How do these appearances strengthen our faith in the reality of his resurrection?

13. Go on to read 1 Corinthians 15:17–22, as well. How does Paul demonstrate how important Jesus's resurrection is to our faith? What is the relation between Jesus's resurrection and the resurrection that *we* will experience as his followers—and what makes this so encouraging to our hearts?

THEOLOGY CONNECTIONS

14. This chapter shows us Jesus eating fish with his disciples and allowing them to touch his physical flesh (Luke 24:36–43); and yet he also suddenly appeared among them, when—as John's gospel tells us—they were meeting in a locked room (John 20:19). When we recite the Apostles' Creed, we affirm the "resurrection of the body." Why is it important for us to cling firmly to the truth that Jesus was resurrected *bodily*—and that we will be too? What seems to be different about Jesus's *glorified* human body? What about his resurrection body remains

mysterious? What can we learn, from Jesus's body, about what our own glorified bodies will be like in the future?

15. Even though Luke 24 does not explicitly address the future resurrection of God's people, we know from the rest of the New Testament that Jesus's eternal life becomes ours, as well, through our faith. Answer 38 of the Westminster Shorter Catechism has this to say about the "benefits" that we receive because of Christ's resurrection: "At the resurrection, believers being raised up in glory, shall be openly acknowledged and acquitted in the day of judgment, and made perfectly blessed in the full enjoying of God, to all eternity." What does this quotation serve to further explain about what Jesus's resurrection means for *you* as his disciple?

APPLYING THE TEXT

16. Do you resonate with the initial doubt that the women in this passage, the eleven disciples, and the two disciples on the road to Emmaus exhibited regarding Jesus's resurrection? If so, why? What about Jesus's resurrection is difficult for you to believe? About your own future resurrection?

17. Why is believing in Jesus's bodily resurrection important to both your own salvation and your eventual resurrection? What habits and practices can you adopt to strengthen your faith and hope in the resurrection life that you will experience in Christ?

18. What encouragement can your study of this passage offer you when you consider the deaths of loved ones and your own eventual death? How could you use the truths of this passage to encourage other believers around you?

PRAYER PROMPT

The event to which Luke bears witness in this passage, Jesus Christ's resurrection from the dead, seals the eternal hope that we place in Christ for our salvation, resurrection, and eternal life. Today, as you close your study of God's Word in prayer, remember that you are praying to God the Father in the name of a risen and reigning Savior. Jesus lives, and he intercedes for you at the right hand of God in heaven. Pray for faithfulness, courage, obedience, and holiness as you follow your risen Savior until the day he returns!

A Word Explains the Deed, pg. 636
We are to believe in the resurrection on the basis of what Jesus said. The empty tomb is not self-explanatory. There is a word that explains the deed, and this word is the gospel message that Jesus not only died, but also rose again with a glorious and everlasting body that would never die again.

Jon Nielson is senior pastor of Spring Valley Presbyterian Church in Roselle, Illinois, and the author of *Bible Study: A Student's Guide*, among other books. He has served in pastoral positions at Holy Trinity Church, Chicago, and College Church, Wheaton, Illinois, and as director of training for the Charles Simeon Trust.

Philip Graham Ryken (DPhil, University of Oxford) is president of Wheaton College. He teaches the Bible for the Alliance of Confessing Evangelicals, speaking nationally on the radio program *Every Last Word*, and is the author of a number of books and commentaries.

Did you enjoy this Bible study? Consider writing a review online. The authors appreciate your feedback!

Or write to P&R at editorial@prpbooks.com with your comments. We'd love to hear from you.

P&R PUBLISHING'S COMPANION COMMENTARY

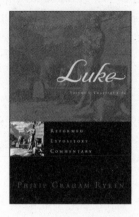

In this commentary, Philip Graham Ryken makes Luke's message clear for a contemporary audience by explaining, illustrating, and applying its truth to everyday life, with the hope that readers will understand the gospel and come to full assurance of salvation, as Luke intended. If an account of Jesus's life was needed in Luke's time, how much more acutely is it needed in ours—and Luke's gospel stands as ready as ever to fill this need.

The Reformed Expository Commentary (REC) series is accessible to both pastors and lay readers. Each volume in the series provides exposition that gives careful attention to the biblical text, is doctrinally Reformed, focuses on Christ through the lens of redemptive history, and applies the Bible to our contemporary setting.

Praise for the Reformed Expository Commentary Series

"Well-researched and well-reasoned, practical and pastoral, shrewd, solid, and searching." —**J. I. Packer**

"A rare combination of biblical insight, theological substance, and pastoral application." —**Al Mohler**

"Here, rigorous expository methodology, nuanced biblical theology, and pastoral passion combine." —**R. Kent Hughes**